Forward

As a sovereign risk analyst for more than 40 years on Wall Street, my career has been extraordinary. I have traveled to 100 countries, most on multiple occasions. I have watched the world change in astonishing ways. I have dealt with governments and their senior officials. I have been at the center of many financial crises.

I have frequently been accused of being at the center of international conspiracies. I was in the World Trade Center for the first terrorist attack in 1993, as well as working and living just a block away from the World Trade Center on 9/11. I have been the object of countless cartoons, and some amusing stories. Some things I have written about have probably never been public.

The reason I have put pen to paper is that many people, after hearing my travel stories and historical anecdotes, have been insisting for years that I should write them down. Also, I am often asked how did I become a sovereign risk analyst? What did I study? Where? This book is my answer to those questions.

The events and people I write about are based on my recollection of those people and events, not on any detailed diary. I never kept a diary. I never thought anyone would be interested in what I did.

Looking back, I find the serendipity of events surprising. I was simply living my life. Until writing this book, I never realized how complicated it actually has been. I can't explain how or why certain things happened, except to see myself as incredibly lucky. Being in such unusual circumstances over so many decades remains inexplicable. I might as well begin.

Growing Up in The Bronx

I grew up in the North Bronx in the 1950s and 1960s. At that time, it was a middle-class area similar to many neighborhoods in Brooklyn and Queens. Most people lived in single-family homes with a backyard. It wasn't *Archie Bunkerland*, but only a small step above.

The neighborhood was a mixture of Italian-Americans, Jews, Irish-Americans and a few other white ethnic groups. We never saw a police car. We left our doors unlocked during the day. At night, the doors were locked. It wasn't Mayberry.

My neighborhood was pretty well segregated. There were very few black families. I can't remember there being any Hispanics. In elementary school, there was only one black student, who joined my class in 5th or 6th grade.

Since we lived near the Westchester County border, a new shopping mall, one of the earliest in the nation, was a short bus or car ride away. It was a combination of middle-class urban-suburban living.

I went to New York City public school, which in the 1950s and 1960s, were excellent. I remember that in 5th or 6th grade, we were given speed reading lessons, something that proved quite useful over the years. It was during elementary school that the schools started closing on Jewish holidays. I was told that it was done because so many teachers were Jewish, so that it made little sense to keep the schools open when so many teachers were absent. My only thought was how really nice it was to suddenly have extra days off in September-October.

On Assembly Days, which occurred once a week, boys had to wear white shirts and ties. At the beginning of each assembly, a teacher read something from the Bible, always the Old Testament. Bible readings ended sometime towards the end of my elementary school career after a 1962 Supreme Court case.

In October 1962, the Cuban missile crisis was at its peak. For years, we had those famous "duck-and-cover" drills, involving either ducking under our desks and covering our heads, or less frequently, going down into the deepest level of the school's basement, which was well below ground, where the coal-fired furnaces were. Looking back, it was probably a safe place to be if a nuclear weapon exploded over New York, but I doubt there would have been adequate food and water for all the students and teachers. These drills were done for purely psychological reasons.

The most fascinating drill was when we were sent home one day and told to locate fallout shelters near our home. Fortunately for me, it didn't take long because there was a fallout shelter across the street from my house, in the basement of one of the very few apartment buildings in the neighborhood. I have no idea how other students fared in their search for a fallout shelter. No one talked about it the next day. Living with the possibility of nuclear war always remained in the background.

Junior high school was quite different. Instead of elementary school calm, excluding duck and cover, I was suddenly thrust into a very chaotic and very different environment. Although there were only three grades, there were thousands of students. To keep order during class changes, there were lines down the middle of each corridor, which you crossed at your peril. The staircases were split between those going up and those going down.

My school was named after John Philip Souza because supposedly, the school emphasized music and the musical arts. It was just another educational experiment. I had no musical talents at all. I never gained anything from the school's *expertise* in the musical arts. More importantly, the Board of Education had what were called Special Progress (SP) classes. The bottom line was that those who qualified for SP status were able to skip eighth grade. That proved a tremendous boon, giving me an extra year to pursue other things.

Junior high school definitely trained me for life in an urban environment. Out of about eighteen students in my SP class, there were no minorities, despite the fact that I estimate about a third of all students in my school were African-American.

I quickly learned to navigate a highly charged racial atmosphere. Lunchtime was the most challenging. I knew a neighbor, who lived down the street, a year or two ahead of me in school. More importantly, he was a real *tough-guy*. He hung out with other really tough Italian-American boys. Looking back, it seems crazy, but one day, I simply went up to his lunch table and asked if he wouldn't mind if I joined him and his friends. In the traditional Bronx accent, he said, "No problem." I was now sitting with the toughest white guys at school. I think they enjoyed the fact that this kid from the SP class wanted to sit with them. From then on, I was never bothered by anyone. Another advantage I had was that I was usually among the taller students in my class, and I always looked older than I actually was. That may explain why I never suffered bullying.

Although my school taught French, Spanish and Italian, if you were in the SP class, you had no choice; you had to study French. I assume it was some educator's idea that French was better for budding intellectuals. Italian was fading fast as Italians were rarely emigrating to the US anymore, while Spanish was viewed as the language of immigrants and the *lower classes*.

No matter what academic program you were in, every student had to take *shop classes*, which were introductions to vocational training.

Besides gym, shop classes were separated by gender. I took metal working, ceramics, carpentry and mechanical drawing. There were still large public vocational schools in New York City. I assume this was an advertisement for those schools. I was never very good at any of these courses. Most things I turned out looked more like art than useful products. The girls took such traditionally *feminine* courses as sewing and cooking.

I vividly remember that I was in metal shop when an announcement came over the PA system announcing President Kennedy had been shot. There was total shock among the students and teachers. Instead of the usual boisterous atmosphere in the hallways, there was near total silence.

We were immediately dismissed from school. No one seemed to worry about whether anyone would be at home if students were suddenly sent home. A different mindset then.

Another required course was typing. This turned out to be among the most useful courses I ever took. It would later make writing research papers much easier. We were told by the teacher that girls would do better than boys because we boys lacked the same manual dexterity as girls our age. We were told it had something to do with *hormones*.

My parents were always indulgent when it came to providing me with anything I needed for my academic career. My parents got me a German portable typewriter. It was great. My mother bought it from one of her colleagues at work. I assume it was one of those typical NY deals, where you could buy things that euphemistically *had fallen off the truck*. In other words, it was possibly/probably stolen by someone. There was never a way to know for sure.

I was an obsessive student. Having a typewriter, knowing how to type and loving history, in 7th grade I wrote a forty-five-page term paper on the Hungarian Revolution of 1956. This probably marks the beginning of my long journey to the world beyond the Bronx.

I assumed I would continue on to the local public high school, Evander Childs. My brother had gone there, and my mother worked there. I was told it would be similar to what I had already experienced in junior high, only on a larger scale.

Anti-Clericalism

One day, my 9th grade English teacher, Mr. O'Reilly, took me aside and said he thought I should go to Cardinal Spellman High School, a brand-new school, just across the street from my junior high. He argued I would have a much better education there than in Evander Childs.

I was not totally thrilled with the idea. Neither were my parents. The problem was that although we were Roman Catholic, my father's family was anti-clerical. The reason for this anti-clericalism was that the region where my grandparents came from was in the Province of

Benevento, which had been part of the Papal States until Italian unification in 1860. Being ruled by the Church was not welcomed. Therefore, despite my grandparents being born about twenty years after Italian unification, family memories of church rule remained. For instance, on occasion, my grandmother would say, "A nun's heart is as black as her habit!" This was said despite my grandmother having a candle lit before a statue of Saint Anthony every single night. God forbid she might run out of candles. Even a blizzard would not have stopped the need for a family member to journey out to buy a box of candles – fortunately there was a little grocery store down the street that carried such things.

Familial anti-clericalism was further advanced when in 1940, my Aunt Ella planned to marry Uncle Phil. In the early 1930s, my family had been among the first Italian-Americans to move to the then bucolic North Bronx. The neighborhood had been predominantly German and Irish. The local Roman Catholic church, St. Frances of Rome, despite its name, was considered by parishioners and the priests to be an *Irish* parish. When my aunt and future uncle went to St. Frances to arrange for their wedding, the Monsignor told them that they would be better off going to St. Anthony, a parish a few miles away, which was considered an *Italian* parish.

Sure enough, they were eventually married at St. Anthony's. The distaste for our local parish always remained just below the surface. That explains why my brother and I did not attend St. Frances of Rome's parochial school.

Mr. O'Reilly had put us in a challenging position. Would we let anti-clericalism close off the possibility of going to Cardinal Spellman? It was touch and go for a while.

Finally, it was decided that my mother and I would take a tour of the school.

The school had a peculiar arrangement. It was co-institutional, not coeducational. That meant the boys remained on one side of the building, while the girls remained on the other side, separated by a large interior courtyard. Both sexes shared the lunchroom. It wasn't that the nuns couldn't teach boys; they could. It was the brothers who were not allowed to teach girls. On the boys' side, we had a combination of brothers, diocesan priests and laymen teachers. The girls were taught by nuns and laywomen.

My mother and I were greeted by the Principal of the boys' school, Brother Cassian Gregory. He was a warm-hearted, big man; tall, fit and sporting a crew cut. There was always a smile on his face.

He greeted us in the friendliest manner. He quickly got down to business. He wanted me to go to Spellman. It was a bit complicated because public junior high school went from 7th-9th grade. Catholic schools didn't have junior high schools. Elementary school finished in 8th grade, with high school starting in 9th grade.

Brother Cassian showed us around. The facilities were excellent. He told us that he would create a special curriculum for me. I told him I didn't want to study Latin. Although Latin was required at the time, he said, "No problem." I would continue with French. He said I could add German if I wanted. It was getting very tempting, very quickly.

By the end of our tour and after our conversation with Brother Cassian, we agreed that Spellman would be my next school.

In practice, it got complicated because I would only be taking certain classes with my homeroom class. A student's schedule required remaining with his/her homeroom class, moving together from subject to subject, teacher to teacher. Uniquely, I floated from class to class, enjoying it thoroughly.

French, German and Mandarin

My French class became a bit strained because my French was considered better than the other students. It's probably because I started studying French in 7th grade, while the other students had only recently begun French.

Brother Martin, a rotund man who looked like your stereotypical monk, was my French teacher. He decided that the solution was for me to study on my own in the school library. He thought it less disruptive for the class, and beneficial to me. What a school!

I really enjoyed German class. It was becoming clear that I *really* liked languages.

I should add a footnote here. The public-school educational system had decided not to teach English grammar. I only learned English grammar while learning French grammar. I then finally learned about nouns, verb tenses, adjectives, etc. It's analogous to today when children are no longer taught cursive writing.

I had another great opportunity to study a different foreign language, Mandarin Chinese. The Carnegie Institute was offering free summer school courses in Mandarin at Columbia University. I jumped at the opportunity.

It may seem strange today, but there was a shortage of Mandarin speakers in the US. Chinese immigration had pretty much stopped decades earlier. Most Chinese speakers in the US spoke either Cantonese or Fujianese. *Red China* was a major enemy. The idea was that if you were willing to study Mandarin, you could continue to study it at Columbia during the following school year on a part-time basis. They even said we would be paid to continue studying it.

My teacher was a Mandarin speaker from Taiwan. She was very good, but clearly hated Communism. One of the best lines I remember from her class was when she explained the meaning of country names in Mandarin. When the Chinese heard the name of a country pronounced in its original language, they took a sound from that and translated that sound into a meaning that seemed reflective of the country. For instance, the US was Mei Guo, or beautiful country. Germany was De Guo, or virtuous country. One exception was R Ben, the name for Japan, which means root of the sun. The best was her explanation for the name for Russia, E Guo, or as she explained it; the land of the starving people to the North. I always doubted that, but it clearly demonstrated her intense dislike of Russia.

Mandarin grammar is extremely easy. Mandarin only has four tones, unlike some other Chinese dialects, which can have five or six tones. I found it wasn't too difficult to distinguish the four tones. The end of school test involved having a short conversation with the teacher in Mandarin. It proved easy. I did not continue studying Mandarin, despite its easy grammar and small number of tones, because of the written language.

Chinese characters are not phonetic. One or two characters can stand for any word. Chinese dialects may have different pronunciations for the same character. One dialect may be unintelligible to a speaker of another dialect. However, no matter which Chinese dialect a person speaks, he can read what is written and understand it. If you have ever watched Chinese language TV, you will usually see subtitles. That allows any Chinese speaker to understand what is being said, even if the speaker is using another dialect. Imagine if Europeans could do something similar!

The problem for me regarding continuing to study Mandarin was that I thought I was already too old to memorize all the characters required to be considered literate. Although I was only sixteen, I knew my ability to memorize was weaker than when I was much younger. I was not willing to devote all the time required to become fluent and literate. Decades later, when I was in my forties, I had no desire to learn to read and write Chinese. I merely wanted to communicate better in Mandarin when I traveled to China, so I eventually took private lessons.

After summer school finished, I made my first international trip. Aunt Christine and I went to Montreal to visit Expo '67, a great world's fair. I loved it, especially the fact that Montreal was bilingual. It appeared quite different from the US, but looking back, the difference was superficial, just related to language.

For several years, I had thought I wanted to pursue a career in linguistics. However, despite my familiarity with Italian, doing pretty well in French, studying German and having now studied Mandarin, I concluded I didn't want to translate what others said or wrote. I wanted to be the person being translated. I know it sounds arrogant, but that's what I thought.

My next step was to look into international relations programs at various colleges. It was a pretty easy choice: Georgetown's School of Foreign Service (SFS).

The reasons for choosing Georgetown were myriad. After two years studying in a great Catholic High School, casting aside my familial anticlericalism, I learned to respect Catholic intellectual thought. Since Georgetown is the oldest Catholic University in the US, with its *then* strong Jesuit tradition, it seemed a good choice. The curriculum at the School of Foreign Service was exactly what I wanted. I applied for early admission and was accepted in October.

Georgetown, as was the case with other Catholic universities, only had a small endowment. That meant scholarships were in short supply. My family and I would have to pay the full cost. With help from my parents, a small loan and, earnings from a summer job, I was able to head off to Washington in September 1968. Today, I doubt it would be possible to fund a Georgetown education so easily.

The DeWitt Nursing Home

A friend of my brother worked in Manhattan as a switchboard operator in a new type of nursing home. He asked if I would work there on summer weekends. I said sure. I was lucky to get the job.

The owner of the DeWitt Nursing Home was Dr. Lichtman, a very large and imperious man, but with a gentle heart. He was interested in international affairs. He liked that I would be going to the School of Foreign Service at the end of the summer.

I was used to living with my elderly grandmother, so I felt at ease with older people. This place was incredible. It was a new type of nursing home not only because it had 499 beds on seventeen floors, but it looked just like a hospital inside, except there were no operating rooms. I was told the number of rooms had been limited to 499 beds because of government regulation. Government regulation would soon prove to be quite impactful, and not in a way you might expect.

Although I started out working on weekends as the switchboard operator, I was quickly asked if I would like to work in admitting during weekdays. I was thrilled with that prospect, because Dr. Lichtman paid me extremely well. This was in 1968, and I was paid about $160 a week, a very decent salary for that era. That made financing Georgetown much easier than it otherwise would have been.

I always thought that my job as an admitting clerk would have been perfect for a pre-med student, but I was quite happy to remain there. I would return every summer throughout my Georgetown years. Dr. Lichtman was so accommodating that he even allowed me to work during Christmas breaks. I owe him a lot.

It was not easy admitting people who were often quite sick and on stretchers. As I learned what the different diagnostic abbreviations meant, I quickly realized who was likely to die soon, and who had a good chance of being discharged. Looking back, this was a lot for a seventeen-year old to absorb. It certainly gave me a new perspective on life.

Getting people to answer bureaucratic questions, and more importantly, getting them to sign the required papers, was a challenge. I remember chasing stretchers down the hall to make sure the documents were complete. I tried to maintain a professional attitude even when I thought I was living in the midst of absolute chaos. In such a big institution, lots of people were constantly being admitted and discharged, often at around the same time.

My colleague, Mrs. Zurko, originally from Hungary, was a delight to work with. She was very elegant, always dressed perfectly, with lots of jewelry. We got along great. I learned over time that she had been forced to go to work at her rather advanced age (I'm going to guess in her sixties) because her husband had unexpectedly died prematurely. As often was the case, Dr. Lichtman, who knew Mrs. Zurko and her husband, came to the rescue by providing her with employment close to her upper East Side apartment.

We both worked for a truly driven woman, Mrs. Weiner. She looked like she could be an Eleanor Roosevelt double. She drove Mrs. Zurko and I crazy. We did what we could to avoid her, which proved difficult. I don't ever remember her saying thank you, or that we had done a good job. It just wasn't in her.

Everything you have seen on TV medical dramas is what I saw at DeWitt. The nurses and other staff had such complicated lives, living in ways I had never witnessed before. Seeing death and sickness all around changes you. They lived outside the norms of society at the time. They were cultural pioneers in many ways. At a time when interracial couples were still uncommon, there were several such couples among the staff. Some of the staff were openly gay. Some male nurses were extremely effeminate. Today, they would probably be considered transgender. The head of the back office was gay. He was not closeted and was not your stereotypical gay man. These were new insights into the greater world.

I never saw any overt discrimination at DeWitt. Race, gender, age seemed to make no difference, something that was still foreign to the world outside this medical center. It was how people treated each other that counted the most. Some were real pains in the neck, but the point was their actions determined how we judged them, not externalities.

There were definitely various levels of snobbery, most often based on education and wealth. This was only obvious after spending time there. Doctors represented the top of the pecking order. No one crossed doctors, even when the nurses knew more than the doctors did about a particular patient. Registered nurses (RNs) were a step above licensed practical nurses (LPNs), who were above nurses' aides. The bottom of the pecking order was the maintenance staff. Utopia it wasn't.

One of the best examples of snobbery was a registered nurse, who looked as if she had stepped out of Vogue. She had an upper-class American accent, which is not often heard anymore. She seemed to look down on almost everyone. What people didn't know was that she needed to work because she was divorced and needed the extra income. No one was to know. She made sure she never left the nursing home in her uniform. She felt she had to make sure no one on the outside would know she worked there. God forbid if one of her neighbors would see her dressed as a nurse! I thought that truly sad.

Besides all the people I met and interacted with at DeWitt, it was fortunate for me that the nursing home was just a short walk to the Metropolitan Museum of Art. I would go there during my lunchbreak almost every day. At that time, there was no admission charge. It was free.

I had a great time wandering the museum halls. Imagine being able to stop by the museum every day over several summers! It provided me a great education in the arts. At that time, we didn't have mass tourism. It may be hard to believe but on weekdays around noon, in the summer, the museum was never crowded. When I returned there on many occasions later in life, I was appalled by the cost of admission. Yes, they say you don't have to pay if you can't, but that's just nonsense. I would never have gone there on a daily basis if I had to give a "donation" every time I went. I would have felt too guilty about not giving, and I certainly could never have afforded it.

Time and again, I have been shocked by how mass tourism has made so much of what I was able to experience impossible to mimic today, not just at this museum, but in tourist sites around the world.

One of the craziest parts of working in *Admitting* was locating the *missing* dead bodies. A nursing home this big and with so many very infirm people was a totally new concept. State regulations had not moved quickly enough to address new problems such an institution posed. The biggest problem was that New York State did not allow a nursing home to have a morgue. This was sensible when nursing homes were small with only a modest number of people staying there. In DeWitt, this simply didn't work.

At first, the staff tried to bring the bodies down to our records room on the first floor, near the admitting office.

However, the main medical record keeper didn't approve of that at all, and she was some tough lady. No one would mess with her. One minor lesson she taught me was that medical records used to be kept only in pencil. The reason was that pencil never faded, while ink did. (An example of more useless information I kept tucking away, only God knows why!) Less important than the objections of our medical records keeper, was that it would violate state rules if a single room became a *de facto* morgue.

Most rooms were shared. Bodies of the deceased could not stay in their room for long. The nursing staff would gather the person's possessions and put them in a plastic bag on top of the body, and then wheel them out on a gurney. Now the adventure began. What would the staff do with the body? They hid them. The most common place to hide the deceased was in local stairwells. Patients and visitors didn't use the stairwells. The staff wouldn't be shocked by seeing a dead person on a stretcher there. This was not a big problem during the day and early evening hours when the coroner's office or a funeral home would be able to quickly pick up the bodies.

The problem emerged at night when no one was available to pick up the bodies. When Mrs. Zurko and I arrived at work, we were given the night's death count, and hoped we could quickly find the locations of the bodies if they were still being hid. It was macabre, but it was necessary.

The most unusual missing body event happened on a Monday morning. The person had died Sunday night. The physical therapy floor didn't open on weekends. Therefore, a resourceful nursing staff member thought the best place for the body would be on the physical therapy floor.

At times, the physical therapy staff needed to curtain off the area where they were working on a patient. On this Monday morning, a young physical therapist was having her coffee when she gently leaned against a table shrouded by a curtain. Suddenly, she realized that something was on the table. When she pulled open the curtain, there was the dead body. She fainted straight out. She was down for the count.

We had a special floor for people who were *senile*, the term generally used then. The 9th floor had the usual patients you would expect to find there. One of the most memorable events happened when a nurse walked into a room with two beds. One of the two gentlemen sharing the room wasn't there. She asked the other patient where his roommate had gone. He calmly said, "Out there," pointing to the window. The nurse panicked. As the nurse soon learned, yes, the other man had gone out the window. His roommate wasn't phased in the slightest. After that tragedy, I assume windows were bolted shut. However, for Mrs. Zurko and me, it was simply par for the course; just another day.

We also had another man on the same floor who decided that he was going down the laundry shoot. Sure enough, he was later found on top of the laundry piled high in the basement.

There was one small Sicilian woman who didn't appear senile to me. She was hunched over in a way similar to many other elderly women in the nursing home. She slowly shuffled across the floor in large oversized slippers. Her face was craggy. She had several moles on her face, with hair visibly growing from them. Her voice was deep and scratchy. Although, I didn't speak any Sicilian dialect, I could understand many things she said. I never fully understood why she was there, but she was, and she would live there for many years. One day, one of the floor nurses said that they caught her throwing salt at her roommate. I knew exactly what she was doing. She was using a traditional Italian curse to drive out her roommate. I don't remember if it worked.

While working at DeWitt, I always wore a sports coat and tie, even when commuting was extremely uncomfortable in the days before air-conditioned subways. I knew that dressing the part was important. Also, it made me look older than I actually was. Having jet black hair and a five o'clock shadow each day also helped.

Georgetown

When my first summer at the nursing home was over, I headed off to Georgetown. The 1968-69 academic year was the last using the old system of starting after Labor Day and finishing after New Year's, which simply ruined the Christmas holiday period because you had to study for final exams. The following year, the academic year began at the very end of August and lasted until mid-December. That gave us about a month off before returning to school, which was a big improvement.

The academic education I received at Georgetown was excellent, but the real learning experience involved simply being among a phenomenal group of professors and fellow students. At first, seeing how differently people lived compared to my own life, was jarring.

During the school year, I did volunteer work at my local Congressman's office, Congressman Mario Biaggi. As a teenager, it was fascinating going into the Capitol office buildings. It all seemed very important to an impressionable teenager (I had only just turned seventeen several months before). However, it wasn't the volunteer work that impacted me most, but rather an encounter with one of the secretaries.

When I arrived to do some office work, which I thought to be very profound, I was told that Angela's father had recently passed away. Like me, she was Italian-American, originally from the Bronx. As I was taught, after someone dies, you offer your condolences to family members. I dutifully walked over to her desk and began to say how sorry I was to hear the news about her father. After asking how she was doing, her response floored me. Instead of the usual "Thank you," she said, "Although my father was just 54, I have to say, he couldn't have done more in his life."

Wow, what an epitaph! I thought to be remembered that way was incredible. From that day forward, I decided I was going to try to live my life with that in mind. My philosophy of life became, "Get on with it!" Do something; don't just sit around and waste your allotted time on earth. Little did I realize how impactful that mindset would be.

Life at Georgetown was **not** a microcosm of America at all. With scholarships scarce, most students came from upper middle-class Roman Catholic families. A sizable portion came from extremely wealthy families. Some girls would arrive with trunks of clothing, not just a few suitcases. Some Latin American students brought their polo ponies! Only a small proportion of the students were not Roman Catholic.

I am not going to bore you with all the details about my academic studies, except when I thought they were meaningful. I had great professors at Georgetown, some more memorable than others.

One professor who stood out was Carroll Quigley. He was an unusual man. His course was the only course EVERY student in the School of Foreign Service had to pass in order to graduate. It was a course about civilization. However, it really wasn't a course about civilization per se, but rather it was a course on how to think, something far more valuable. He taught us how to organize mega-subjects into divisible parts, thus enabling us to make a cogent argument surrounding almost any issue.

His exams were unusual. We would have three questions that had to be answered in about an hour. It was the nature of the questions that made it so *challenging*. I remember one question was to trace the role of women in Anatolia over a millennium. Another question was, "What was so important about the 5th century BC?" Each had to be answered in about 20 minutes.

Detailed knowledge was not important. Rather, everything depended on how you could organize an incredibly complex topic in just a few minutes.

Quigley was viewed by us as a kind of *force of nature.* His commanding lecture style, combined with the backdrop of Georgetown's famous Gaston Hall, provided added *gravitas* to the subject matter.

You may not have heard of Gaston Hall, but you certainly have seen it on countless occasions, because it's often the site for major political speeches. It's great for television.

My Modern Foreign Governments class was taught by Professor Jeanne Kirkpatrick. Her behavior was definitely noteworthy, if only because she gave the entire course sitting at a table on a dais in the front of the room while her legs were seemingly spread out in all directions, with her hands waving demonstrably. There was nothing sexual about it at all. Only later did I learn that she was dealing with alcoholism. In the future, after she gave up drinking, whenever I saw her, her demeanor was totally different. That's why she proved to be such a good US Ambassador to the UN.

She told great stories during class, which always related to the topic at hand. I remember two of her stories quite well. She had lived in Paris in 1958, a pivotal year in modern French history. The Fifth Republic was about to be born, as De Gaulle tried to end the chaos of the Fourth Republic, and finally bring the Algerian crisis to a close.

She said she saw an advertisement in the Paris metro. The ad was for Duron Paint. On the poster there were three young ladies dressed in Empire-style gowns. They appeared to have just left a theater stage. Then, there was a fourth young woman, who was half on-stage and half off-stage. The first three were labeled the 1st Republic, the 2nd Republic and the 3rd Republic. The fourth woman coming off the stage was labeled the 4th Republic. Then below the image, the following line was added: *Republics come and go, but Duron Paint lasts forever.* In French is sounds even better because the name Duron is a play on the French word *to last*. Professor Kirkpatrick said this amusing advertisement used during a major political crisis was indicative of how the French were able to mock themselves, showing a strong sense of what it is to be French.

Her next story about that turbulent period was a joke, which she said was making the rounds in Paris in 1958. It went like this: A man goes into a bookstore and asks for a copy of the French Constitution. The clerk says he's sorry, but the bookstore doesn't sell periodicals!

All in all, I loved both stories, and have told both of them countless times over the years -- I'm sure much to the chagrin of my listeners.

Another professor who had an unexpectedly big impact on me was my professor of modern European history. I regret I can't remember his name, but I do remember he was Cuban-American, with a strong Spanish accent.

When we got to the Spanish Armada, he simply opened his remarks with "The tragedy of the Spanish Armada…" I was blown away. Obviously, from a Roman Catholic perspective, the defeat of the Armada by the Protestant English was an historic tragedy. On the other hand, I had always been taught in school how great it was that the English were victorious over the Spanish in 1588. That one passing comment made me realize, for the first time, how pliable history was, and usually written by the victorious. Instead of rejecting the study of history, I became even more enamored of it. Later, when studying in Italy, I become familiar with the writings of Benedetto Croce. I found his insight into history seminal. Croce considered the study of scientific history farcical. He believed only philosophers should write history.

Reading history provides an insight into human behavior. How people interpret their past is a good indicator as to how they might interpret and react to contemporary events. This proved useful when doing country risk analysis. Knowing how a country interprets its history helps to better understand how a government might react to contemporary events. If you can understand how a country's elite interprets history, you may have a useful tool for predicting their future behavior.

After freshman year, I went back home and again worked at DeWitt. While working during the day, in the evenings, I took Economics 101 at Fordham University. The professor made the subject matter so fascinating that by the end of the summer, I had decided to major not just in international affairs, but I would take enough electives in economics and mathematics to be able to go straight into a graduate economics program.

By far, my favorite Georgetown professor was Mme. Mikus, one of my French professors. She was really my mentor. She was very opinionated, and clearly right-of-center, a place I wasn't at that time in my life. She was from Besançon in Eastern France in the Jura region. I still remember her very high-pitched voice, which added a special charm both in English and French.

I learned so much from her about European culture, and European history. Her husband was also a professor, but at a different university in DC. I recollect that he had been a Czechoslovak diplomat prior to the Communist takeover. Now, he was vehemently anti-Communist and was a proud Slovak nationalist. Before meeting him, I hadn't even thought about Eastern European nationalism. It just wasn't on my radar. Also, in addition, it was only after meeting both Professors Mikus did I begin to learn about the pivotal role Roman Catholicism played in shaping 20th century European history.

I often dined at their home. Both were perfect representatives of all that had been good in Europe. The conversations around the dining room table were always enlightening.

Professor Mikus was fully convinced that Slovakia would eventually become independent. It was something difficult for me to imagine. Decades later, when Czechoslovakia shed its Communist regime, and more surprisingly, the Czech Republic and Slovakia split apart amicably, Prof. Mikus and our talks immediately came to mind. It's just further proof that anything is possible if people genuinely believe it possible.

In my freshman year, I lived at the International Students House (ISH) on the East Campus. It was a building dating from the pre-Civil War period. We were told that during the Civil War, the main floor, which was a few steps down from the entrance, had been a morgue. It was said that the upstairs rooms had been used as a residence for nurses.

My fellow dorm residents were truly an eclectic group.

My first roommate was Eloy Cerpa, a student from Mexico who, along with his brother, was studying English at Georgetown. I was told that his father headed the federal police in his home state of Chihuahua. Even at that time, it must have been an *interesting* job, putting it mildly.

One day, Eloy told me that when I spoke directly to him, he could understand me quite easily. However, he said when I spoke with friends, the speed of my English increased so much that it was pretty unintelligible to him. That taught me to pay closer attention to the linguistic skills of others, which proved quite useful in later years when giving speeches in English to non-native English-speaking audiences.

In my freshman year, the biggest hit book and movie was *The Exorcist* by William Blatty, a Georgetown alumnus. Although the original story behind the book did not take place in Washington, Blatty used Georgetown as the backdrop for the story. What made this extra special was the house where the exorcism was supposed to take place was right across from my dorm. Although there was some artistic license used in the book and the film, the house and the infamous stairway were nonetheless there to see every day, albeit located somewhat differently from the movie. It certainly added atmosphere.

Although Stonewall occurred just after my freshman year, being openly gay was still unusual and positively risky. On the positive side, my Constitutional Law Professor Giles was pretty much known to be gay. I had heard that, on many occasions, the school would have to bail him out of jail because of the severe legal restrictions on gays at that time. I had to give Georgetown credit for not firing him, despite the fact that Georgetown was a Catholic University. That was pretty progressive for the late 1960s.

On a sleazier note, across from our dorm was another dorm, whose windows faced ours directly. The room that faced those of us on the third floor had three guys sharing one room. Very quickly they started to have gay sex pretty much out in the open, for anyone to see. Hard to avoid seeing them because the windows were only separated by about 10 feet. Unlike what might have happened in other schools at the time, no one made a fuss. We simply ignored them and went on with our own business.

Most of my dormmates thought I would flunkout because they never saw me studying. What they didn't know was that I woke up very early, at least for a student, usually at about 6:30 AM. I then studied several hours and was then done for the day. I never left assignments for the last minute. Unlike many of my friends, who woke up late and then studied late into the night, I was able to watch TV and relax in the evening. Hence, they assumed I would fail. Well they were wrong.

Although dorm life was fun for the first year, many of us had grown tired of the small, enclosed space each of us had. Also, the school cafeteria was a bit of a hike, especially during inclement weather. We could cook in our rooms, but in the days before microwaves, the most we could have was a hotplate. We thought it would be nice to have a regular kitchen.

1420 33rd Street, N.W.

Six of us got together and rented a townhouse in Georgetown at 1420 33rd Street, NW, between "O" and "P" streets. It was a big old three-story house. We rented it from a Mrs. Simmons, the widow of a former Chief of Protocol during the Eisenhower administration. She was a lovely lady who oozed protocol and formality.

She told us that she had been born in that house on the desk on the second floor, which was still there. Eventually, I wound up in that room. I could never fathom why or how she came into the world on that desk.

Our landlord quickly had repairs made to the house prior to our moving in. However, she informed us when we visited her in her Dumbarton Oaks home to sign the lease, during the winter she couldn't be reached because she "wintered in India" (pronounced by her as Injjia, with a strong accent on j sound). Therefore, if we needed anything, we should simply contact her live-in maid. Mrs. Simmons proved to be a delightful landlord for the several years that we rented her townhouse.

The prior tenants proved interesting. They were young women who worked on Capitol Hill or on political campaigns. One of the women was closely involved in the Chappaquiddick scandal. She had been hounded by the press.

After moving in, we found a little black telephone book, the infamous kind. In it were the names of some of the most important Democrats in DC, including the number for Teddy Kennedy. This was in a period before the partisan divide became toxic. What did we do with the little black book? We threw it out. It was the right thing to do.

We had also interesting neighbors. Dan Rather, then at the top of his career, lived just across the street. A few houses up from us, Averill Harriman and his wife Pamela had their townhouse. You get the picture, it was a pretty upscale neighborhood.

There are several things to keep in mind about Washington, DC in the late 1960s. The riots following Martin Luther King's assassination destroyed a large area of DC, especially around 14th and U Streets. DC was crime-ridden. At night, it was dangerous to go anywhere east of Rock Creek Park. Even the area around George Washington University and Foggy Bottom were considered unsafe after dark. Rock Creek Park provided a geographical divide that lasted for many years. Some may find it hard to believe, but even Dupont Circle was dangerous, day and night. It was considered the center for the drug trade in Northwest DC. Dupont Circle is quite different today. Capitol Hill was then a lawless *frontierland*, which some brave people were just starting to gentrify. Union Station was an eyesore and falling apart inside.

The years 1969-1970 proved to be extremely important regarding opposition to the Vietnam War. At the time, although I was not sure about the war, I was still uncomfortable with the idea of actively opposing the government.

My housemates had diverse opinions regarding Vietnam. Two or three of them actively opposed the war. Then in November 1969, one of our more politically active housemates, Mark Vermillion, asked if we could let some people stay over for a major demonstration. I was not thrilled with the idea. However, after much coaxing, Mark and my other housemates convinced me to say, yes. I made only one demand, and that was that no one was to share my bedroom.

In retrospect, that anti-war demonstration proved to be the largest anti-war demonstration to ever take place in the US. Estimates are that half a million people peacefully descended on DC. Despite my protests, I wound up having 7-9 people sleeping on my bedroom floor. They were well behaved, but the more than 50 protesters staying with us proved to be the physical limit for the number of people we could handle. In addition, because the number of people coming to DC was so large, there were short-term shortages of food in local stores. By the end of their short overnight stay with us, all our food and drink supplies were depleted.

Since our *houseguests* came from all sorts of backgrounds, they were quite surprised with how well we lived in this big old house, with fireplaces in every room.

That protest proved to be simply the start of protest after protest. However, unlike the initial November 15th demonstration, in the future, protests became more violent.

The house parties were extraordinary. It was a time when drugs were ubiquitous, especially marijuana and hashish. Both were always *free*. I was told that most of it was brought in by the children of diplomats in the diplomatic pouches.

I can remember that party goers often brought trays of Alice B. Toklas brownies. It was only after attending several parties did I realize that the brownies were laced with marijuana, and hence got their name. In many respects, I was naïve, to say the least.

Alcohol flowed everywhere. Mostly it was wine and beer, though on occasion, there was some hard liquor.

One of the extra-curricular evening classes at Georgetown was a wine and cheese tasting class, taught by the local wine merchant who owned a store on Wisconsin Avenue. Since we were studying at the School of Foreign Service, it seemed appropriate that we should learn all about fine wine and cheeses. It was certainly one of the most entertaining classes I've ever taken. In all fairness, it was quite instructive. However, the real fun came at the end of the class. During the actual wine tasting we were only given small amounts of each wine. As the evening wore on, the wine bottles would accumulate at the end of each row of desks. Once done, the class simply drank all the wine that was left, which was considerable. The cheeses added to the atmosphere. Believe it or not, that wine tasting class proved quite valuable over time. With more than a passing knowledge of wines, it added to a perception of sophistication. However, I can't help but smile when I remember how I had learned all that.

As a result of one party, I met two young female French students. We became friends. One lesson I learned from them was how to make crepes. It was so easy to do, but really impressed people. I used that bit of culinary knowledge to provide quick late-night snacks on numerous occasions over many years. I still always have a proper crepe pan in my kitchen.

As the school year passed, the tension over the Vietnam War steadily increased. Demonstrations occurred on a regular basis. On April 30, 1970, everything began to spiral out of control. President Nixon announced the US was invading Cambodia. That meant that not only was the war continuing, but it was escalating. That's when campuses across the country exploded into mass demonstrations. On May 4, 1970, when Ohio National Guards killed some students at Kent State, campus tensions reached a fever pitch across the nation.

On several occasions, national guard troops were posted on every street in Georgetown to protect Georgetown residents. We had one very nice soldier who stayed in front of our house. Of course, we were nice to him. After all, he was about our age, and probably just went to another college.

Things became very hectic even on the Georgetown campus. It became difficult to get to class. The chaos reached such a crescendo, that final exams were suspended, and if I recollect correctly, we were given pass/fail grades that semester because there didn't seem to be a better alternative.

Perugia, Italy

I had planned to spend my junior year abroad in France. When I arrived in France, for reasons, which I still don't fully understand, I didn't want to stay. Before going home, I traveled to Italy. That first trip to Italy marked another turning point.

When I crossed the Italian border, I felt indescribably *at home*. Everyone looked like they could all be relatives. Coming from a multi-ethnic, multi-racial country to one where my own ethnicity was ubiquitous was strangely overwhelming. It made me feel more comfortable about myself. I would no longer be susceptible to the stereotyping of Italians and Italian-Americans, which was common at the time.

I returned to Italy for my second semester, enrolling in the Università per Stranieri in Perugia. Once again, I plunged into a different world. Yes, everyone looked like me, but Italians lived and looked at the world very differently from what I was used to.

I spoke reasonably good French and understood most Italian because I had heard my grandmother use her Italian dialect. My parents also spoke Italian, but it was their second language and as with my grandmother, it was based on a version of the Neapolitan dialect used in the 19th century. They used Italian when speaking to my grandmother or when they didn't want me and my brother to understand what they were saying.

Although my grandmother understood everything I said in English, she would always only answer in Italian. My father explained that when Nonna (Grandma) was younger, she had tried to speak English, but when people made fun of her attempts, she simply stopped trying. That was a real shame.

On my arrival in Perugia, I went to the university's housing office to find a place to stay. After introducing myself, the woman behind the desk looked at me and smiled. She then told me she had a great *pensione* for me. The problem was that the *pensione* owner wouldn't rent to Americans. She said Signora Campanelli might make an exception because I looked like a nice Italian-American boy. After a brief phone call, I got the go-ahead to check out the pensione, or rather, for Signora Campanelli to check me out.

To walk to the pensione from the university I had to walk through Perugia's famous *Arco Etrusco*, an archway dating from Etruscan times. I learned later that despite some remnants from Etruscan times, Perugia is better known as the only major Gothic city in Italy, or so the *Perugini* claimed.

It was a long climb up one of the many steep hills in the city to get to the Via dei Priori, which would become my home in Italy. It was a totally medieval looking street. Narrow, with very old buildings lining each side, I finally arrived at my destination. I was struck by the size and quality of the doors at the entrance. I soon observed that, in Italy, you can often tell the wealth of residents by their outside doors, since it was usually impossible to tell just by looking at the outside walls.

Signora's pensione was three flights up a marble stairway. On arrival, she looked me up and down, and I got a nod of approval. She showed me my room, which I would be sharing with an Italian university student, who I soon learned was a member of Italy's Fascist Party. I was definitely not in Kansas.

The chaotic continuum of Italian political beliefs amazed me. Here my roommate, Giovanni, was a Fascist, while I learned that Signora Campanelli, who watched out for Giovanni like a son, was a Communist. I was never sure if she was a true believer because I was told by other residents that she was a Communist out of respect for her long-dead husband who had been a member of the Communist Party.

If she was a Communist, she was certainly the most capitalist Communist you could imagine. Her business acumen was phenomenal. She had built this pensione in order to feed her family. As a widow after the war, there were few ways a woman could earn a decent living. Owning a boarding house was one of them.

She started out small, but after decades, she now had this beautiful two-floor pensione, with about a dozen guests, most of whom were staying there for months, if not for years at a time. The residents were overwhelmingly

Italian. There was one family, the *Ispettore* and his wife and daughter. The Ispettore was the equivalent to the head of a board of education. They were living there while their new condominium apartment was being built. The Ispettore was elegant. He was soft-spoken, and always curious about things. Despite all the great conversations we had, the one thing that sticks in my memory was how he ate a banana. Italians usually hate to eat things with their fingers. The Ispettore would carefully chop off both ends of the banana. Then he simply slit the skin, and *voilà,* the banana emerged from its shell in one piece, which then allowed the Ispettore to slice small pieces and eat them with a fork. Form was and is extremely important to Italians.

The only other foreigner besides me was a young Japanese student, who the Italians told me spoke near-perfect Italian. She was also quiet as a mouse. I still don't know how she was able to walk down a wooden staircase within the pensione without making a sound.

There was one absolute rule in the pensione, and that was posted on a sign in Italian in a prominent place in the dining room, which was the main focus of the residence. In Italian, it said, *Here, we speak only Italian!*

For me that rule was a bit difficult at first, since I had yet to learn much of it. Looking back, I'm sure that rule helped me to learn Italian so quickly. Although my Italian vocabulary was quite limited at first, I was able to regale the other residents with my version of a series of amazing insults said in my version of a Neapolitan dialect. They would roar with laughter, not because I was saying it incorrectly, but rather they told me I had captured the Neapolitan dialect all too well. They often asked me to repeat the string of insults. A Neapolitan dialect and accent are Italy's version of a Yiddish accent. Both are closely associated with some of the best humorists in their respective cultures.

The Signora provided room and board, including three meals a day with wine at lunch and dinner, as well as laundry service. All the really hard work was done by *la donna*, obviously a peasant woman. Despite coming back several times over the years, I never learned *la donna*'s actual name. She simply scurried about, always doing something.

Everything was taken care of by La Signora and *la donna*. In the early 1970s, Italy was much poorer than the US. My monthly rent for all these services was an amazingly low Lit. 60,000, which at the time was less than $100. Today, Italy is as expensive, if not even more expensive than the US.

There were a few things that took getting used to, one of which was taking a shower in the pensione. Energy prices were exceedingly high, even in this pre-Arab oil embargo period. Hot water in sinks and the bathtub was only available on an as-needed basis. For the sink, you turned on the water and then turned on the electric heater which immediately heated the water. Before taking a shower, you had to turn on the water heater in a tank above the bathtub. It took about 20 minutes to get the water hot. If you went even a few drops beyond the amount of the tank's capacity, the water became instantly cold, something not appreciated in a cold bathroom in mid-winter.

There was a central heating system, but once again, because energy prices were so high, it was used sparingly. It seemed to go on for short periods of time during the day and night. When it was really cold, La Signora would light a Franklin stove in the dining room. It really helped heat the room quite well. Best of all, it was fired using wood. The smell of the burning wood was quite nice. Since other homes had similar sources of heat, when you walked outside during the morning and early evening hours, the air was often filled with a pleasant smell of burning wood. To this day, I remember that scent with fondness.

The university was great. It taught Italian using an intensive approach. The professor I had was a character. He was a slightly balding middle-aged man, who was constantly on the prowl for young women in his classes. His aggressiveness was jarring, because although the US was far from developing a culture where men were as chivalrous as required by today's PC world, his behavior was still over-the-top even by then extant US standards.

Despite his lack of great looks, he seemed to have been quite successful in his pursuit of young women. I have to admit that he was an excellent teacher. Within a month, I was speaking reasonably good conversational Italian.

That broadened my interactions. The conversations around the dining-room table became more interesting. One young student named Luca was studying art. His closest friend at the pensione was a young student, Laura, whose father was a successful doctor. I eventually learned that Luca's family came from an old aristocratic Tuscan/Umbrian family. Obviously, no family is *older* than another -- we all have to have the same number of descendants. Social background was key.
There were definite class boundaries, not usually crossed by Italians, among themselves. As a foreigner, albeit an Italian-American foreigner, I was exempt. Until I learned to speak more and more Italian, these boundaries were not evident to me, nor to any foreign casual observer.

A sidebar to social snobbery was how Italian aristocrats viewed British aristocrats. We Americans certainly have seen British snobbery, if not in practice, then in the theater, in movies, or on TV. It always seems that British aristocrats look down on everyone else. What I found in Italy made me smile. As one young Italian aristocrat told me, "The British aristocrats are just parvenus. We were noble and sophisticated when the British were still crude; eating with their hands, while we were using forks and knives." That was certainly a surprising new perspective for me to ponder.

Giovanni, my fascist roommate, was fascinated by his American roommate's views. I learned more from him about fascism then I could ever have taught him about capitalism. He was also the first person I had ever met who was completely into conspiracy theories, something that was not yet so influential in the US.

It was from him that for the first time I learned about genuine fascist philosophers, such as Giovanni Gentile. I had never heard of Gentile before. In Florence, he is buried in a place of honor in the grand Basilica of Santa Croce.

When I went back to Georgetown, I found there were many books by him and about him in the Georgetown library. I wondered why I had never been presented with his ideas in any class. Although fascist, he was considered by many as the best neo-Hegelian philosopher of the early 20th century.

After reading some of the seminal fascist writers, I learned how easy it would have been to adopt a fascist ideology. This is not the fascism portrayed by the Nazis. Some Italians argued that if Mussolini had not joined with Nazi Germany, Mussolini might have lived as long as the other two long-lived fascist dictators, General Franco and Portugal's Salazar.

The fundamental idea behind theoretical fascism is that society's main social groups must work together for the greater good, with the government being the final arbiter. As with all great schools of thought, it easily became derailed. Although considered the premier Fascist philosopher, Gentile deplored anti-Semitism. In the end, he was assassinated in Florence, towards the end of the war, by partisans. Ironically his assassination occurred while he was arguing to get anti-fascists released from prison.

In many respects, theoretical fascism shares many similarities to Confucianism.

The historian John Fairbanks provided a description of the difference between Western law and Chinese law. In Chinese culture, traditionally based on Confucianism, Fairbanks argued, everyone is supposed to work *harmoniously* under the guidance of the government, which had a leader who possessed the so-called *Mandate of Heaven*. Historically, it was the emperor who held that mandate. Today, one could argue that it is possessed by the Chinese President.

Fairbanks argued that traditional Western law was based on transcendent rules, which had to be obeyed. Sources for such Western laws would have been based on biblical writings combined with the Roman idea of a written constitutional. Civil laws had to conform to these "natural laws." On the other hand, for the Chinese, law serves society, not the other way around. Law is, by its very nature, malleable. For instance, Chinese contracts need to be adjusted whenever such changes benefit the greater good, with the final arbiter being whoever held the Mandate of Heaven, which means the government.

The Western view of law and the Chinese view result in quite different reactions to business. The best example I know to illustrate this is when the Beijing government wanted to tear down a MacDonald's restaurant in downtown Beijing in order to build a big new shopping mall. The Chinese said that MacDonald's could have a place in the new mall. MacDonald's said, no, it had a firm contract. Both sides didn't understand each other. They were talking along parallel lines. In the end, the government won out, but not before losing a lot of good will and understanding of foreign investors, who now knew that contracts were not necessarily final. Real theoretical fascists would have had no difficulty understanding the Chinese position.

Another fascinating aspect of life in Italy, at least among university students, was that cafes or *bars*, as the Italians call them, were segregated by politics. Communists went to the Communist bar. Fascists went to the Fascist bar; so on, and so on. To an outsider, you would never have known which, was which. They all looked the same.

Italy's bar culture was also something new to me. Italian bars can provide alcohol of any sort, but I rarely saw any Italians drinking alcohol in the bars. In the early years, I don't remember seeing a single Italian drunk on the street, or even in private. This has unfortunately evolved over time.

People drank wine, usually mixed with water, during their meals, but never to excess. In bars, coffee was consumed, with most taking just small cups of espresso -- certainly not the wild coffee drinks we have created in recent years in the US with all sorts of Italian-sounding names. In the morning people would often have a coffee and a biscuit of some sort. There was nothing elaborate.

In the pensione, breakfast was usually caffé-latte, or half warm milk and half coffee. Alongside, there would be small slices of hard, leftover bread, with butter and marmalade.

After living in Italy for a few months, I missed an American breakfast of cereal. I bought some in a local store, which catered to the many foreigners studying in Perugia. I brought it home to the Signora who was happy to give it to me the following morning.

When I sat at the table, she then brought in a bowl of cereal, not filled with plain, cold milk, but covered in caffé-latte. I smiled and thanked her, because I knew she was trying to accommodate me, without knowing how cereal was normally eaten. Looking back, it was my fault. I had expected she would know what to do with cereal, when Italians, at that time, knew nothing about it. Needless to say, I didn't ask for cereal again.

I surprised my Italian friends and the Signora because I had a credit card and I had personal checks. None of them had heard of a credit card, despite the fact that credit card logos were displayed on many shop windows. Credit cards would not become ubiquitous in Italy for many years.

Campus Craziness

I returned to Georgetown in the Spring of 1971. Things had become much crazier in the US during the so-called 1971 May Day demonstrations. I missed the worst of it because I was only just returning from Perugia. I only saw the immediate aftermath. I heard countless stories from my friends who were actually there.

I was told that even Carroll Quigley was threatened. During that time, for protection, he regularly brought his large German Shepherd with him to class.

I was also told that the Georgetown campus was tear-gassed. I'm quite glad I missed all that action. Hearing about it was more than enough. The May Day 1971 demonstrations in DC were the most violent demonstrations in Washington's history. Some argue that the government's actions were the closest Washington has ever come to establishing martial law broadly across the city. If anyone even looked radical, they would often be arrested, just in case. It certainly set the tone for Nixon's growing paranoia.

One more humorous story involved a fellow student who had a very nice sports car parked on 33rd Street, NW. When he heard noise on the street, he looked out the window and saw his small sports car being lifted up by a group of demonstrators using it to block the street. He was then heard yelling out the window that he was for the revolution, so please leave his car alone. The *mob* didn't listen.

I could have graduated in December 1971. However, since the draft was still in effect, and since I had received a low number in the new lottery system, I hoped to postpone being drafted as long as possible. Therefore, in January 1972, I went back to Perugia.

Life in Canada

Before returning to Europe, I applied to the graduate economics program at McGill University in Montreal. I had many reasons for choosing McGill. Montreal was a bilingual city. I really liked that. Also, McGill had a great international reputation as Canada's premier university. In addition, it followed a different academic pattern than US universities did. It was a mix between the British tutorial system, used so effectively at Oxford and Cambridge, and the American system based on credits. That simply sounded great. However, the final decision was determined by cost.

I would be finishing Georgetown with very little student debt. My parents had helped me pay for Georgetown, but I would and should pay for grad school. McGill was incredibly inexpensive, even for foreigners. Tuition was about $600. I calculated that I should be able to finish all the requirements for a master's degree in one academic year. Therefore, beyond the small tuition, I only needed to fund my living expenses. This was doable, especially since I was able to get into a graduate dorm on the McGill campus, which provided full room and board. That meant most costs were knowable in advance. Also, even though I would be studying there on a student visa, I only had to pay about $80 per year to be eligible for the Canadian health insurance program. For me, it was a no brainer.

Also, I knew it would take a few months after graduating before I might get drafted. One academic year might prove short enough for me to finish my master's degree before being drafted. You couldn't receive a draft exemption for grad school.

At the time, and for many years later, my having studied in Canada during the height of the anti-war movement was clearly on people's minds when first meeting me, but absolutely no one ever asked me about that. Several of my professors at McGill had indeed moved to Canada to avoid the draft. It was quite common.

Once more, fate intervened. I went to meet my graduate advisor, Professor Loutfi. At our initial meeting, he asked me why I hadn't applied for financial aid. I answered that since I was a foreigner, I didn't think I would be eligible. However, his response pleasantly surprised me. He said I would be eligible to be a teaching assistant. As a result, McGill University paid for the four years of my education there.

Although, now I could continue on with my studies without concern about funding, I still had the draft hanging over me. During the summer after my first year at McGill, I went back home, and back to work at the nursing home. That's when I got my draft letter. I went for the physical. I assumed I would pass. However, surprisingly, I failed. As a result, I no longer needed to worry about being drafted. Another example of how life can turn on a dime. I had been preparing to serve in the military, and had planned my life around dealing with that, and in one day, those plans changed entirely.

I was now free to continue my graduate education, going as far as a doctorate, if I so desired.

When I returned to McGill in September, now that I was better funded with money saved from working at the nursing home and a second year as a teaching assistant, a former dormmate and I rented an apartment in what was then called the *student ghetto,* an area where inexpensive apartments could be found just a short walk from campus.

At the end of my first year of graduate work, I successfully passed the written test required to get my master's degree. However, I then needed to write a master's thesis, something not often required in American universities.

School work proved demanding. It required endless hours of reading academic articles, usually about arcane areas of economic theory. I can't say that I enjoyed it, but I knew it had to be done. What really helped me a lot was being a teaching assistant. That meant that I would meet with students, and in my case, I retaught them everything they needed to know about Economics 101. That exercise forced me to make sure I really understood what I was teaching. That helped me enormously to truly understand economics.

Another benefit of being a teaching assistant was that I became used to public speaking. I've been giving speeches and doing presentations ever since, or for more than forty years. As time passed, it became easier and easier to teach, give presentations or simply give speeches. Without that grounding as a teaching assistant, I doubt it would have proved so easy.

My master's thesis proved more difficult than I had imagined. It wasn't hard to do the economics. What proved extremely difficult was the actual writing of the thesis.

My thesis advisor was Prof. Loutfi. He might have been an excellent professor, but he and I didn't work well together. He hated my writing style. He criticized it so much, that I began to doubt my ability to write. Everything was beginning to get jumbled in my mind. My progress came to a standstill.

My good friend Don encouraged me to continue to write, no matter what Loutfi said. He then suggested getting an editor if necessary.

At first, I took up his suggestion in getting an editor. She helped somewhat, but really, I still didn't see what I had been doing wrong before. Since I didn't see the work produced by the editor was very different from what I had written, I slowly, very slowly, concluded that it was not simply my problem. It appeared to me that Prof Loutfi was a major contributing factor to my writer's block.

I decided the best way to deal with this was to find another thesis advisor, which I did. Professor Graham, an economic historian, came to the rescue. He was so easy to work with. I explained the problems I had been having with Prof. Loutfi. Prof. Grantham slowly rebuilt my confidence. With his gentle guidance, I was able to complete my thesis and get my master's degree, albeit a little later than I had first anticipated.

My experience with Profs. Loutfi and Grantham taught me another valuable lesson. Do not let one person destroy your self-esteem. If someone is doing that, even if inadvertently, ask for help. A simple change in my thesis advisor resulted in major progress in my academic career.

Brazil to the Rescue

I wish I could say that it was a quick process in getting Loutfi out of my head, but it wasn't. I wanted to escape from all the pressures of graduate school. I was fortunate to have enough money saved so that I was able to go on a vacation to Brazil in January 1974. I found a student group from the Boston area which was going to Rio for three weeks. They needed some extra students to help keep the charter price down. I jumped at the opportunity.

That proved a God-send. January is the Southern hemisphere's equivalent to July in the North. It was summer in Rio, while Montreal was steeped in another horrible winter. Arriving in Rio, my gloom lifted.

Beyond that psychological benefit, I was now getting some experience in Latin America. This would be the first of many trips to Brazil over the decades.

In the mid-1970s, Rio was nowhere near as dangerous as it would later become. Our hotel was just a short stroll from Copacabana beach, and a short taxi ride to Ipanema. It was safe by the beach, and even inland was relatively safe, except late at night. We were able to take the cable car up Sugar Loaf at night, something which in later years became very risky.

Since the other students had classes to take while in Brazil, they were not as free as I was. I took advantage of that vacation. I booked a flight to Brasilia, which was then still being completed. The government moved the capital from Rio because it wanted to make Brazilians look more towards its vast interior, rather than simply living along the coast.

I remembered how strange the city appeared compared to Rio or any other major capital. It was totally sterile. I thought the attempt to be modern was excessive. The city was laid out in the form of an airplane. Different neighborhoods were devoted to different functions. The sidewalks were eerily quiet during the day, nothing like Rio.

The architecture was monumental and not very attractive. The only memorable building was the cathedral.

My next trip was to Sao Paolo. It was spectacular, and huge. It reminded me of a Latin American version of New York, with skyscrapers everywhere. It was and still is the business center of Brazil. It was much more European than Rio. There were fewer Afro-Brazilians living there. You could tell that there were lots more people of Italian, Spanish and Portuguese origin.

One thing I learned early on was to take tours of cities I was visiting for the first time. I always learned a lot, and if I returned in the future, I would know which places to explore further.

In Rio, I had already done just that, and was fascinated to learn more about Brazilian history. When touring Petropolis, once the capital of Brazil, I learned the Portuguese king decided to move his capital from Portugal to Brazil following the devastating Lisbon earthquake of 1755. I was surprised to learn that Brazil was the only country in Latin America that had a colony in Europe.

Seeing the tropical side of Brazil was fascinating. It was incredible that I went from Rio along the coast, to a tropical paradise outside Rio, to Petropolis, a city in the hills near Rio, but with a much cooler climate. The houses in Petropolis appeared as though they should be in Switzerland. It was definitely a land of contrasts.

One of my favorite stops in Rio was the Opera House. There was a museum there with a large collection of Carmen Miranda memorabilia. There was a mannequin all decked out in a wild costume she had worn in one of her famous films, including her iconic hat made of various fruits piled high on her head. Only then, did I learn that she was actually from Portugal, and was considered one of the best fado singers of her time. Fado is considered the true soul of Portugal. It's definitely haunting music. That's an important reason why Carmen Miranda was in the museum, not simply because of her film costumes.

There was another oddity in the museum, and that was a mink coat or mink stole. It was in the museum to show that despite being quite warm in Rio, even in the Southern hemisphere winter, some elegant women, including Carmen Miranda, wore furs to go to the opera. I found all this absolutely fascinating.

When in Sao Paolo, the tour included huge auto plants along the highways. As an economist, the number of factories really impressed me. A little further outside the city, we saw examples of the famous coffee farms, found in the rolling hills. To this day, and after many trips to Sao Paolo, I'm sorry to say that I don't remember any iconic symbol of the city itself.

From Sao Paolo, I visited Sao Vicente, a resort along the coast, close to Sao Paolo. I was told wealthy Paolistas spent their weekends along the coast, with one of their favorite places being Guaruja. A close friend's family, who I knew from Georgetown, had one of their main family residences in Sao Paolo. His family had made lots of money from cashews. He told me that his father used to fly by helicopter from their apartment in Sao Paolo to Guaruja because the traffic was intolerable. Not such a bad life.

When back in Sao Paolo, I visited with my Brazilian friend, Geoffrey Brandt, who maintained his main Brazilian residence in Rio. He invited me over for lunch. It was a magnificent apartment. The lunch was rather formal, with the maid providing a great Brazilian meal. Many years later, when I was living in New York City, it turned out that a close friend of Geoffrey lived right below my apartment. Coincidences never seemed to end. Years later, I heard Geoffrey died prematurely from cancer.

After three weeks in the sun and warmth of Brazil, I was ready to plow back to my academic work in Montreal. I often wonder how I might have coped with all the stress I had been under if I wouldn't have had the opportunity to go on that three-week vacation.

Winter in Montreal

I returned to a brutally cold Montreal. I should say that despite living in New York City, and having visited Montreal during the summer of 1967, I had no idea how cold and snowy the city would be. The first year I arrived at McGill, in early September 1972, the weather was already peaking in the mid-40s. It went downhill from there. The first snow arrived on October 9th. The first time it went below zero Fahrenheit was on American Thanksgiving. Throughout this book, I rarely can give you exact dates for particular events. However, on these dates, the weather and temperatures are all permanently etched in my memory. I never got used to Montreal's winters.

"Mon pays, ce n'est pas un pays, c'est l'hiver." The English translation is, "My country is not a country, it's winter!" This one line from a well-known Quebecois song summed up Montreal's weather.

In recent years, the weather in Montreal seems a bit warmer than in the 1970s. Perhaps my memory of it exaggerated the cold. Nonetheless, the coldest temperature I experienced in Montreal was -33C. That is super cold, or the equivalent of -27.4F. The wind chill was off the charts.

At the same time, no matter how cold it was, life in Montreal seemed to go on as usual. There were miles and miles of underground shopping malls and underground passageways connecting the metro to the malls and the malls to each other. To get from the McGill campus to the nearest *inner earth* metro station was just a few blocks walk above ground. On the campus, all the buildings were connected to each other through countless subterranean passageways. I quickly learned all the various routes required to keep myself indoors as much as possible.

I still wore glasses. I wouldn't start using contact lenses for many years. Eventually, about twenty years ago, I had lasik eye surgery, which proved transformative. With glasses, going from a bitterly cold outside to a warm and toasty inside caused my glasses to fog up until they warmed up. It was really annoying.

Another thing I had to get used to was that I always needed to wear boots. The boots were usually either muddy or, more likely, wet with a mix of salt and snow. Whenever you went into your own home or someone else's, you left your boots outside the door on rubber mats. What most surprised me was that I never heard of anyone having had their boots stolen from the outside halls. Stealing someone's boots was the modern Canadian equivalent to horse steeling in bygone centuries.

While I lived in Canada, the country was just switching to the metric system. That was a challenge for everyone. However, I still remember how the government tried to make it easier for people to convert Fahrenheit to centigrade in their own head. It was a simple, but ingenious approach. Most people don't really think about what each degree of temperature actually represents, but rather, what impact it might have on them.

The first thing that comes to mind is that temperature determines what outer clothing we wear. We all knew what 32F felt like, and what clothing that would require. We were told that freezing using centigrade was equal to zero. At 5C, you needed to wear a warm jacket or a lined raincoat. At 10C, you needed a slightly lighter jacket. At 15C, you only needed a light sweater or very light jacket. At 20C, you no longer needed a jacket. After that, it simply became warmer and warmer, requiring less clothing. It became pretty simple. Individual readings overall were far less important than the five-degree multiple. It still works for me. It was always easier to think in terms of below freezing in centigrade, because it just meant that we kept adding more and more layers of clothes, which in Montreal at the time, was a challenge.

Despite the weather, I enjoyed living in Canada. It was similar to the US, but it also had some interesting quirks. The quirkiness was, by far, larger in Quebec. The mid-1970s was a time of on-going and often raucous debates about the role of the French language in the province. The Parti Quebecois (PQ), the party for Quebec independence, was formed in 1968. It kept gaining political strength in the National Assembly (the provincial legislature with a grand name). It wasn't until 1976 that the PQ formed its first government. When that election occurred, I was not living in Canada, but temporarily in Ireland.

67

Dublin, Ireland

How did I wind up in Ireland? That came about as a result of my returning to McGill following my trip to Brazil. I was still jolted by the weather, and also by the stress related to writing my thesis. I thought it would be a good time to take a break.

By then, I had been to Europe on several occasions for various periods of time. I thought about finishing my graduate studies in the UK. In those days, it was inexpensive for a foreigner to study at a British university. I was accepted at the University of Manchester. However, by chance (once again), I saw an advertisement in the Economist magazine for a Ford Foundation-funded assistantship at Trinity College in Dublin. The research project was to study public enterprise in the smaller Western European democracies, which described Ireland quite well. It would be a great learning experience, and I would be paid to do it. Fortunately, with my slowly growing resume including studying international affairs at Georgetown, economics at McGill, foreign languages and a growing list of countries I had already visited, I was accepted.

I took a leave of absence from McGill. I was off to Dublin in September 1974.

Ireland in 1974 was quite different from what it is like today. Most noticeably, it was far poorer. There were only the Irish and some British people living there. Foreigners were rare. I had heard that in the West of Ireland, Germans were just beginning to buy country homes. I never met any.

I stood out because I have an olive complexion. Today, Ireland's population is so diverse, I would no longer stand out. I would not want to give the impression in any way that I ever witnessed a single act of discrimination or unkindness against me. I guess being Italian-American put me many steps above the still disliked British. In the 1970s, *The Troubles* were still raging in the North.

I was able to rent a room at a house in northern Dublin, close to Glasnevin cemetery. It was in a new, small development of shining white houses, with small gardens in front and back. The owner of the house was a young man who had recently completed his MBA at Columbia University. He had bought the house and was helping to pay it off by renting out the extra bedrooms. The accommodations were comfortable. Also, my landlord and the other tenants were all about the same age, with similar interests. In addition, next door there was another house similarly rented, but this time to young women, most of whom were working in normal jobs, including one stewardess who worked for Aer Lingus, the national airline.

Aer Lingus stewardesses wore green stockings. That caused a problem when they flew to Denmark because there, according to the next-door neighbor, wearing green stockings was an outward sign of a *woman of the evening*.

That wasn't the kind of advertising Aer Lingus or its stewardesses wanted.

It was only a short bus ride to the center of Dublin. From there it was about a 10-minute walk to Trinity. The bus stop in downtown Dublin was eerie. Just before my arrival in Ireland, the IRA had bombed a monument to Lord Nelson, which sat at the end of McConnell Street. All that was left now was a stump. *The Troubles* were never really far from people's minds.

One advantage of living with people who were already beginning their careers, was that several of them owned cars. This made traveling around Dublin and Ireland, in general, much easier than it otherwise would have been.

When I went to Trinity College to meet the two professors in charge of the project, I found them both quite pleasant. The office where I worked was on the second floor of the main entrance to the college. It was to the right, above Trinity's iconic archway. The view from the window was stunning. I looked out at the famous internal quadrangle, with its incredibly well-manicured and vibrantly colored green lawns and Trinity's bell tower.

Trinity was certainly historical. Founded by Queen Elizabeth I in 1592, Trinity College has had many famous alumni. The list includes such stellar names as Jonathan Swift, Oscar Wilde, Samuel Beckett, Bram Stoker, etc. You get the picture. It's a great place of learning.

The Trinity library has the world-famous *Book of Kells*, an illuminated manuscript dating from about the year 800 A.D. It contains the four gospels plus some other commentaries and is primarily based on the Latin Vulgate translation of the bible undertaken by St. Jerome in the late 4th century.

Not surprisingly, given who founded Trinity, it was considered Ireland's Protestant university. This had some minor impact on day-to-day things. Ireland banned contraceptives. However, Trinity had signs up on its bulletin boards indicating where women could get *cycle regulators*, an obvious euphemism for birth control pills. That would not have gone down well in Ireland's Roman Catholic colleges.

The academic work was not the most interesting part of living in Dublin. As usual, what interested me most was seeing how different the world could be depending on where you lived.

You've already heard me complain about the weather in Montreal. Dublin had its own *charming* weather. The first three weeks I lived in Dublin, it rained every day, for part of the day. That didn't bother me much because after a brief rain, unlike much of northern Europe, where the sky can remain grey for weeks on end, the clouds always seem to be racing across the Irish sky providing some sunlight, even if for only a short time.

The house where I lived had central heating. Since I only had two pairs of shoes, the challenge the rain posed was getting my shoes to dry out. Every night, I would put my shoes under the radiator and hope they were dried out in the following two days. They usually did.

Social life centered around the pub. Irish pubs were different from British pubs in that Irish pubs were less well-lit and more like American bars. Rather, I suppose, American bars are mirror images of their Irish origins.

I loved watching Irish TV. The really odd thing was that although everything was censored in Ireland in those years, we had access to British TV, either from the North or from Wales. BBC was far more risqué than American TV in the 70s. So, we had this ironic situation where there were censored RTE broadcasts, at the same time, we had risqué and controversial programs from BBC beaming into Irish living rooms. It reminded me of the irony of the *cycle regulator* problem.

Besides TV, all films were censored. In a movie theater, before a movie began, a page of information written in Irish was shown indicating who had censored the movie. Since I didn't read Irish – I never heard it called Gaelic in Ireland – my friends had to tell me what it meant. After you had seen one censorship form, the others were pretty easy to recognize.

I was usually able to watch the 6 PM news on TV. Prior to the news, at precisely 6 o'clock, there was an image of the

Virgin Mary holding Baby Jesus displayed on the screen. Then the bells toned, marking the Angelus. I enjoyed the 6 PM ritual. The news in English followed. After the English language news came the news in Irish, spoken by the same announcer. Even I could tell from some borrowed English words, that both news broadcasts were the same.

The only other occasions I was confronted with the Irish language was on bus signs. Destinations were only written in Irish. I quickly learned the Irish words for destinations such as *City Center*.

When I asked my Irish friends about Irish, it was explained that everyone had to study it in school, and that you had to speak Irish in order to be able to teach. It seemed a shame to me that the use of Irish had fallen away so much in modern Ireland. As I noted, we would get TV from Wales. Welsh was being far better preserved than Irish. I recently learned that the use of Welsh is beginning to rise.

My recollection of watching Welsh TV was that when there were public announcements or the news in Welsh, the language had a lilt to it that was very distinctive and quite pleasant to the ear. It was much easier to listen to than Irish. Welsh sounded like a language that the munchkins would have spoken if they were real. I mean no insult by that comparison. That's just what always came to mind.

Although I have usually found languages easy to study, I never attempted to learn Irish. I didn't have a good ear for the language, because even when I would imitate what others said in Irish, they said my pronunciation was terrible. In the end, as my grandmother decades before, I simply put no more effort into it.

On many occasions, the Irish government had advertisements on TV which proclaimed: "Be modern! Say, no, to the rounds system!"

At first, I didn't know what that meant. It soon became clear. If you went to a pub with five friends, or met them at a pub, you were socially obligated to buy each of them a drink and drink what they bought you. I quickly learned to order the smallest glasses of beer, to reduce the possibility of having a hangover the next morning.

The government's interest in ending the rounds system was that not only did it cause far too much alcohol to be consumed, but since alcoholic drinks in pubs were quite expensive, working-class families might see the husband waste a good portion of his salary on drinks both for him and his mates. Not a good idea.

I shouldn't make you think that this was related to social class. It wasn't. At Trinity, there was a bar on campus that opened in the morning. By noon, many students were clearly either drunk or getting close to it. I have never seen more drinking than what I witnessed in Ireland. When I left Ireland, I always joked that *I had to have my liver laundered*.

At the same time that alcohol was consumed on a major scale, a large percentage of the population wore little pins on their lapels indicating that they had taken *The Pledge*. That meant that they had given up drinking. There were many who wore such pins. Since so many people did not drink, any per capita measure of Irish drinking would be terribly skewed by the number of abstainers. That meant the rest of the population drank even more than per capita figures would indicate. Similar problems occur throughout Northern Europe and the former Soviet Union.

The Irish respected other people's privacy. That translated into no one bothering you, unless you gave some indication that you would like to chat. Once you seemed willing to chat, you would then have found yourself having a great conversation with a total stranger. I found the friendliness of the Irish to be their most endearing quality.

If you remember my comments about Italy, you will know that Italians are very class conscious, standoffish and often extremely rude to each other. Italians treat foreigners in a friendly manner, but that doesn't extend to their own people. The Irish, on the other hand, seemed genuinely friendly, not just to foreigners, but to each other. I don't want to exaggerate the point, but I think you understand what I am getting at. An Irishman would have a far better chance of speaking with another Irishman even if he were to visit a pub for the first time. If an Italian went to a bar where he wasn't known, it is extremely unlikely that he would be able to have a conversation with another Italian, nor would he want to speak to the others. Of course, there are always exceptions.

There was one thing that was difficult to get used to in Ireland. That was, no one would say, "No." My best personal example was when I would bring my laundry to be washed. I would leave them with the shopkeeper. I would invariably ask if the clothes would be ready that afternoon. She would invariably respond in a thick Irish accent, "Twill surely be ready this afternoon!" The problem was, she had no intention of having the clothes ready by then. As I learned from other Irish people, I was supposed to understand when her "Yes," obviously to them at least, she meant "No." I was told that people just didn't want to hurt your feelings by being negative, so it was thought better to avoid the blunt truth. You may notice, I didn't say, lie. It wasn't really a lie because I was supposed to understand what her response really meant. I got used to it and simply accepted it.

Professor Chubb was a well-known political scientist. Although not a presidential election year in the US, I always diligently voted by absentee ballot. When I showed him my ballot, he was amazed by its complexity. Unlike most election ballots around the world, the US ballot can be quite complicated, not simply with many political parties no one had ever heard of, but for all the positions that were elected, including judges. Beyond the election of local and state leaders, there were a number of ballot measures, which required a, *yes* or *no* answer. My legal residence was still technically in New York City. That year my New York ballot was about two feet by three feet. Professor Chubb was in awe. Before that, I had never given any thought to the fact that our elections differed so much from other democracies.

There were two trips within Ireland that are still etched in my memory. The first was a visit to former neighbors who had retired back to their hometown of Ballina, on the border between Counties Mayo and Sligo. The McLaughlin's were delightful people. Their sons remained in the US. I contacted my former neighbors when I arrived in Ireland. Of course, I immediately got an invitation to visit them.

I went there in November. I had to take a train to this far western part of Ireland, beyond the Shannon River. Although the distance was not great, the train ride took many hours. The further west we went, the wilder the land looked. The beautiful rolling hills around Dublin eventually turned into rugged plots of land. By the time I reached Ballina, I felt like I had reached, not just the end of Europe, but the end of civilization. I imagined this is how people must have felt about this place before the discovery of the New World.

It was bleak and somewhat unhospitable. The weather was far more volatile than in Dublin. The clouds moved ever faster across the sky. It was much poorer than the Ireland's East coast. The seacoast was dramatic. There were large cliffs facing an ocean riled almost constantly by strong winds coming out of the West. These winds were no gentle Gulf Stream breezes, which warmed Cork and even Dublin. Instead, along the beach there were huge boulders seeming to be dropped from the sky. As my hosts told me, these rocks were thrown there by the sea. The power of the ocean in these parts was extraordinary. They appeared quite different from what glaciers often leave behind. These were not ancient objects. They could have arrived on those beaches in recent years.

It rains a lot in the West of Ireland. Despite that, there were billboards with calls to conserve water. Despite the heavy rain, the nature of the soil and the lack of adequate reservoirs meant that water was often in short supply. This became clear when I first stepped into the McLaughlin home. They had a very modern house. The center of the house was the kitchen. In the kitchen, instead of a simple gas or electric stove, it contained a large peat-fired stove which included a large oven. It was beautiful. When it was used, the kitchen quickly became nice and toasty, something I would soon learn to cherish.

The McLaughlin's informed me that although they had modern, central heating in the house, because of the problems with water supply, they had to keep it turned off so as not to destroy the system. Given the local weather, which was very cold, and very damp, some sort of heating was necessary.

After some homemade scones and homemade bread, we ventured out to meet some of their relatives. On arriving at the home of one of the relatives, I was immediately given the place of honor. This house didn't have modern central heating, or if it did, I didn't notice any signs of it. However, in the main gathering room, there was a huge fireplace, and I mean huge. The place of honor was to be seated almost inside the fireplace. The fireplace had all the utensils needed to cook over the fire, attached to the interior walls. It was incredibly comfortable to be seated there, not far from the glowing embers.

I was regaled with all sorts of traditional Irish treats. They were so friendly, trying everything to make me feel more comfortable.

As nighttime fell, we were off to the local pub. It was definitely the heart of the local community. It was filled with people enjoying a Saturday night out. There was laughter all around. That's when I noticed for the first time, that I didn't really understand a lot of what was being said. I don't think they were speaking Irish. However, the accent was now so extreme that I only understood a few words. The McLaughlin's and their relatives had been used to speaking to people from beyond Ballina. I could easily understand whatever they said. However, the locals who most likely had not lived abroad or in Eastern Ireland were probably only used to hearing their strong local accent. This reminded me of my experience at Georgetown with my roommate Eloy. He understood me when I spoke directly to him but didn't understand a single word I said when I was speaking to American friends.

All of this would have been enough to make the trip to Ballina memorable. However, what followed next made it truly unique.

When we arrived home, the McLaughlin's said that they would light a fire in my bedroom in the fireplace. Also, they asked if I might want to have them heat the bedsheets with special bedwarmers. I foolishly said it was unnecessary. I told them I was used to the cold in Montreal. I was sure I could manage. Frankly, I didn't want to make any more work for them. Then the saga began.

When I pulled back the heavy blankets and the sheets and got into bed, I realized that because of the extreme dampness and the constant chill, it was like getting into a wet bed. If anything, the bedclothes made me feel even colder than if I hadn't used them. After a few minutes of freezing, I got up and slowly started getting dressed. Eventually after several attempts I wound up not only getting fully dressed, but I also put on my overcoat. I still didn't feel comfortable. I had a pretty sleepiness night.

That experience taught another lesson; listen to locals when they give you advice on how to deal with their local situation. If I had only listened and allowed the McLaughlin's to make a fire in the fireplace and to warm my bedsheets, I might have had a good night's sleep instead of waking up chilled to the bone. Never did I feel as cold in Montreal, through all the really rough winters, than I felt that single night in Ballina.

My second memorable trip was over the St. Patrick's Day holiday. At that time, St. Patrick remained mainly a religious holiday. As Patron Saint of Ireland, his feast day meant a day off for everyone. I was told there would be a small parade in Dublin, but that it was absolutely nothing like the parades in Boston and New York. My friends who had lived in the US said it was not worth staying in Dublin to watch the parade.

It was decided that a group of us flat mates from both next-door houses would drive to County Donegal, in the far northwest of Ireland. By chance, the weather in Donegal proved much kinder that weekend than my earlier stay in Ballina. We had lots of sun and gentle breezes. Nonetheless, the terrain was as rough as what I had seen in Ballina. It wasn't the actual stay in Donegal, but the drive to get there that was memorable.

Since my friends all worked, we left on a Friday afternoon. That year, St' Patrick's Day fell on a Monday, perfectly timed for a three-day weekend. We wouldn't be going via any major highways. It would prove a complicated drive at night. The main event was when we arrived in Omagh, a small town in the North, on route to northern Donegal.

We were getting lost. We had already gone through British checkpoints once we entered Northern Ireland. We had no trouble getting through them. We had another checkpoint before reaching Omagh.

In May 1973, there had been an IRA bombing in Omagh, which killed British soldiers. In June, another bomb exploded, but this time it involved IRA deaths resulting from a premature bomb explosion while driving. There was tension everywhere we went in the North. Barbed wire, soldiers, checkpoints were par for the course. We had security checkpoints in the Republic, too, but they were few and far between.

The streets of Omagh were deserted. Nothing was open, not even gas stations where we might have gotten directions. We have to remember that this is in pre-GPS days.

Then we suddenly saw and elderly couple walking down a deserted street. We thought they might be able to help. I will never forget their reaction when we pulled the car up next to them. They both nearly jumped a foot in the air. They were absolutely terrified. We all felt horribly about frightening them so badly. As the only American in the car filled with the others with their southern Irish accents, I became the spokesman. I believe hearing my American accent calmed them a bit. I then carefully asked for the directions we needed. We drove off and left these two stunned people standing there unmoved on the sidewalk. I am convinced they thought that when the car stopped next to them, they would be shot by gunmen. That event colored the rest of the weekend for me.

My friends explained that this part of Donegal was a hotbed of IRA activists. Even though we would not have been their targets, it certainly didn't make me feel any more comfortable knowing there were guerrilla forces all around us, out-and-about, *in plain sight*.

My work on the project passed uneventfully. However, I was becoming antsy to get back to McGill to work on my Ph.D. That Spring, I told the two professors that I would soon be returning to the US, and then to Canada.

McGill

I really didn't want to return to the nursing home, despite the good pay. I let some of my friends know that I would be looking for a summer job. One friend I knew at Georgetown found me a job at the World Bank, in the area which gathered stats on the Eurodollar market. It was a bit of drudgery, but once again, I was continuing to bulk-up my resume.

When I returned to McGill, I wound up sharing an apartment with another student, who I had not met before. He was in pre-med. He had a two-bedroom apartment just a short walk from the economics department. The only catch was that he required me to abide by his kosher kitchen laws. I agreed.

I knew something about kosher laws from my youth in the Bronx. I wasn't yet completely familiar with all the requirements, but it proved to be easy to do, especially since the kitchen was equipped to keep kosher. The biggest thing was to keep meat separate, in every way, from dairy products. I was told, but can't be sure if it's correct, that the reason was that God didn't want any animal to be cooked in its own mother's milk. That sounded good enough to me.

We had separate dishes, cookware, glasses and utensils. It really wasn't a burden to maintain kosher laws. My real takeaway from that experience was that keeping kosher made me think about religion every time I ate or cleaned up anything. It is a powerful reinforcer of Jewish tradition for Jews and was simply a reminder for me about religion.

That academic year centered around preparing for my Ph.D. oral exams, the toughest part of getting a doctorate. I believe I had some seminars and continued to be a teaching assistant. Preparing for the exam was totally nerve-racking. Most of the academic year was a blur.

When I finally got to the Spring semester, I was as ready as I would ever be to take the exam. I knew that a high percentage fail the first time. I had to prepare myself for possible failure. Professor Grantham was incredibly helpful in getting me ready for the exam.

When the day of the exam finally arrived, I was completely wound up. So much work and effort had gone into this. It was the most nervous I have ever been, before or since.

I still remember my first question. Derive the supply curve for factors of production from the social welfare function. To this day, I don't know how my mind was able to answer that in a satisfactory way. I don't remember anything after that first question. In the end, I passed. I was on autopilot. I couldn't really settle down for about one week after the exam. Writing it down now is the first time in decades that I have thought about it. I guess, despite passing, it was just too stressful to keep high on my list of memories. Sometimes we prefer to bury unpleasant memories.

Soon after the oral exam, I went back to Europe for an extended visit. I was really adding more and more countries to my international checklist.

The following academic year, I was going to devote myself to writing a doctoral dissertation. However, for some reason, I just wasn't interested in doing that. Was it that my memory of the master's thesis and all the aggravation that entailed was still too fresh in my memory, or did I simply not want to continue with academic studies? I don't know the answer.

I do remember speaking with the chairman of the economics department. I asked why it seemed to take so long for any of our McGill graduate economic students to complete their doctorates. His response blew me away. He said, "What difference does it make, since you will be doing the same thing for the rest of your life?" That really wasn't satisfactory to me.

Charlotte, North Carolina

I intended on doing things, not just analyzing things for purely academic purposes. I decided to see if I could find a job in economics. At the time, Mr. Cordell was the only *headhunter*, I could find dedicated to finding jobs for business economists.

I called him and asked if I could meet with him during the upcoming Christmas break. He agreed.

When I went to his Wall Street office, I found that he worked by himself and was handicapped. As he sat across his desk, he told me that it was almost impossible for him to find a job for someone just out of graduate school. He said not having a doctorate wasn't a problem. Completing everything but the thesis (ABD – All But Dissertation) was viewed positively by many firms because they really didn't want academic economists.

He offered me coffee. As he began to get up, his handicap became obvious. I said I would take care of that. I got both of us our cups of coffee. I believe that one small act of kindness shown to him may have had an incredible effect. We chatted some more. As I left, he said he would keep me in mind. I assumed I would never hear from him again.

Then just a few weeks later, he called me in Montreal and said that a small bank in Charlotte, North Carolina was looking to create a country risk department, and that they were willing to take someone directly out of graduate school to set it up. Wow, what a shock in so many ways!

First, a bank was willing to at least consider me for a job. Second, where on earth was Charlotte, North Carolina?

The bank was North Carolina National Bank (NCNB), with about $7 billion in assets. At the time, it was about the 25th largest bank in the US. They were just beginning to expand their international business and knew they would need to make sure they had controls in place to assess international creditworthiness. This was especially important because in 1975 the bank nearly collapsed. It made it through with expert leadership. However, regulators and shareholders would keep a careful eye on any new business.

You may find it strange that I wasn't sure exactly where Charlotte was. I assure you, unlike today, Charlotte was little known outside the South. It was not the financial powerhouse it eventually became.

I flew to Charlotte in January. It was a really small city. Today, I would describe what I saw as nice suburban-style neighborhoods even near the downtown area. I saw it as a provincial backwater. When I arrived downtown at the NCNB headquarters, I saw a 40-story skyscraper. It was the tallest building in the city. There were one or two other tall buildings, also owned by banks.

I met the Senior Economist, Al Smith. He was a Columbia-trained economist. He was smart and very pleasant. I spent most of my time with Jim Sommers, the head of the international department. He was smart and quite dynamic.

One of the first questions I was asked was if I could set up a country risk department. I said, "Yes." I could give that response quite forcefully. I had little doubt because no one could tell me I was doing it wrong. Country risk analysis really didn't exist as a specialty. The field was in its infancy.

After meeting with several other people at the bank, Jim Sommers took me to the 40th floor for lunch in the bank's dining room. It was built to impress. It was as nice as any fine restaurant. Jim explained that since the bank had many very religious customers who didn't approve of alcohol, the alcohol was all hidden behind large cabinet doors. It was only displayed when the bank knew it wouldn't cause offense. That didn't make me enamored of Charlotte. It was a perfect example of what living in the heart of the Bible Belt would be like. I had serious concerns about that.

We sat at a table near the huge windows looking out at Charlotte below us. What I saw were miles and miles of trees. It looked less like a city from where I was sitting than when I had seen it while driving in from the airport.

After a few days thought, I turned down the job offer. I was back to studying and teaching in Montreal. The weeks dragged on. Then on one fateful day, and I truly mean fateful, I was walking back to my apartment, this time back in the student ghetto. It was March 15th at about 2 PM. The wind was whipping, and the temperature was -10C (14 degrees Fahrenheit). I had finally had it. I decided I couldn't stay another winter in Montreal. When I got back to my apartment, I called Jim Sommers and asked if the position was still open. He said it was. I told him I would accept it as long as they allowed me to finish my teaching assignments. That meant I would be heading to Charlotte in early May.

My career as an international economist and country risk analyst had begun.

When I left Montreal at the very beginning of May, everything was still bleak. Spring had not really begun. My parents had bought me my first car, an Austin Marina, the summer before. At 25 years old, it was nevertheless my first car. I first drove to New York City to see my family. Then I was off to Charlotte with a car totally packed with all my stuff.

I remember, as I drove South, everything got greener and greener. When I reached Charlotte, after driving about 12 hours non-stop, Spring was in full bloom. Everywhere, the trees and flowers were decked out in all their splendor. This was the same city I had seen as a backwater only several months before. Now I was reveling in being there. Why? Let's just say that our minds are quite malleable.

As I've already written, country risk analysis was in its infancy. There is no other way to describe it. We have to keep in mind how much technology has advanced since the 1970s. With no internet, the only way to gather news was by subscribing to newspapers and magazines. The next task, besides reading everything possible, was to clip articles from newspapers. I spent many hours doing that. The most important source of international news at the time was *The Financial Times*. There was no publication which came even close to the breadth and depth of the FT.

The IMF and the World Bank published data, but the problem was the data they published was *old* and not focused on the statistics needed.

Emerging Market (EM) countries, at the time were labelled Less Developed Countries (LDC). The labels changed over the years, but the same issues, in different guises, remained. Before Mexico defaulted in 1982, EM countries produced very few publicly available data. In Mexico, international reserves were only given during the annual State of the Union speech. Debt numbers, outside those available from the World Bank, were often non-existent. The World Bank debt numbers were limited to government-guaranteed debt and were a year or two old.

Important sources of information were the desk officers at the U.S. State Department along with the IMF and World Bank staff, all easily accessible by phone or by a visit to DC. In the end, travel to the countries was absolutely vital.

Travel

Travel to so many countries over so many years has made my career incredible. Over the decades, I have been to at least 100 countries. I have visited most of them multiple times. I can easily outline most major trips while working at NCNB. Many were first-time visits to those countries, and the number of countries was more limited compared to my later careers at Irving Trust and Moody's. As a result, for my two-year stay in Charlotte, I am able to outline an approximate timeline, something I won't be able to do from 1980 onwards. As noted in the introduction, I never kept a diary of the things I did, because I never imagined anyone would be interested in reading about my travels.

Compared to today, international travel was far more complicated in 1977. Appointments with people had to be made via telex, a ponderous process which usually took at least one day before you received a reply. The same was true for air travel and hotel bookings for EM countries, even though we used a travel agent. On top of that, as soon as you arrived in a country, the first thing you needed to do was to reconfirm your flight out. Many airlines required you to physically go to their office. It was a huge waste of time. Some more technologically advanced airlines allowed you to reconfirm by telephone. Although easier, it depended on the phone service of the country you were visiting. Phone service was intermittent, at best, in most EM countries, something that wouldn't be solved until the arrival of mobile phones decades later.

The next thing you worried about were the required inoculations. Small pox vaccinations were no longer routinely given in the US since 1971. Since small pox still plagued many other countries, the US still required mandatory vaccination for international travel. Then you had to check what the latest additional requirements were for visiting specific countries. Yellow fever shots were often needed. You needed to keep track of DPT shots. Cholera was another disease you might need to be protected against. Then there were other diseases, which although not having a preventive vaccine, still required you to take medicine before and after a trip, with malaria being the most important. Bug spray also helped fight all mosquito-borne diseases. There were many other medical things we all had to keep watch over. I just don't remember them all. When travelling abroad, you always carried your little yellow booklet confirming what vaccines you had, including their expiration dates.

Today, travelers still must be careful when traveling to specific countries or regions plagued by less common diseases. It's just that the list of those countries and regions is far smaller now than it was 40 years ago. Today you can buy over-the-counter medicines for diarrhea. At that time, you needed a doctor's prescription to get Lomotil, the commonest and most effective medicine then available.

Put politely, *intestinal distress* was a constant problem on every trip I took, especially in the early years. As time passed, I guess I became immune to many of the pathogens responsible for it. After about 20 years, the percentage of times I suffered from that fell dramatically, to a point where it very rarely happens anymore on any foreign trips.

The next obstacle when traveling to EM countries was the lack of news in English, or any other language I understood. If the FT arrived, it arrived days after publication. It was old news. I solved this problem by always carrying a shortwave radio with me. First, if BBC was available, I would listen to that. In some parts of the world, BBC came in both shortwave and over the AM network. When BBC wasn't available, I would listen to the Voice of America, which wasn't as good a source of news as BBC. When I got desperate, I would listen to Radio Moscow's English service. Radio Moscow was available *everywhere* but was pretty useless unless you just wanted to know if really major news events were happening.

It was very isolating traveling alone in those first years. As I returned to countries, and as I got to know the places better, the degree of isolation diminished. A sense of isolation on extended trips nonetheless remained until 1989. When visiting Algiers for the first time, I was suddenly shocked to see CNN being broadcast in English in my hotel. Soon, I began to see CNN broadcasts in many other hotels worldwide. The world had suddenly shrunk big time!

While working for NCNB, most of my travel involved Latin America. One of my first major trips was to the west coast of South America. I started in Chile and then worked my way north to Peru and Ecuador.

Latin America

Chile

Visiting Chile in 1977 was an eyeopener. The coup overthrowing the Allende regime happened four years earlier in September 1973. However, the country still looked like it was under martial law. Soldiers carrying machineguns were everywhere. It seemed as though they were on every street corner in the downtown area. My hotel was a big old hotel, famous for its earlier elegance. It was on the same large plaza which contained the then still severely damaged La Moneda Palace, bombed during the 1973 coup. In front of the former Presidential Palace sat a large tank. It wasn't simply on display. It was a serious warning to anyone who might oppose the new regime.

The US embassy was just off the main square from my hotel. I made what would become the usual rounds of speaking with officials at the central bank, the finance ministry, local and foreign bankers plus academics and diplomats from the US and sometimes from the UK. Often the British embassy staff were more knowledgeable about what was happening than their US counterparts.

From person after person, I heard of the hardships at the end of the Allende years. It had been getting dangerous for the middle and upper middle classes. One banker said that the biggest problem he and his family had was getting milk for his small baby and food for his other young children.

I was sure there was another perspective on the coup. However, it was obvious to me that a large number of people supported the coup, if not explicitly, then at least tacitly. In 1977, Chile was returning to normalcy. At the same time, the country was undertaking a grand economic experiment. It was in the midst of adopting economic policies advocated by University of Chicago professors. Chilean Chicago School alumni quickly became leaders in Chile and began to transform the economy. It didn't happen quickly. It would take decades.

On a subsequent trip, I asked a Chilean economist why investment was so low? He answered that famers were beginning to plant fruit trees and grape vines, which would take years to mature. GDP statistics do not consider the long gestation periods for trees and vines to produce fruit. Once they matured, the benefits would become obvious because GDP measures output, not patience.

The government was also helping the farmers to arrange for the proper storage of their crops, as well as for vintners to have access to the best technology, which came from California. The result is that now we can find Chilean fruits, vegetables and wines in most supermarkets in the US and around the world. Before the coup, Chile was only known for copper.

The government began a program of creating what we would call today a rainy-day fund financed from copper sales. Since commodity prices are volatile, the government wanted to make sure that during periods of high prices, money would be saved, which could then fund expenditures during periods of low prices. Despite all the ups and downs of the copper market over the decades, the Chilean scheme has worked pretty well. In all fairness, I should add that Chile has the lowest marginal cost copper in the world. Therefore, Chile is able to profitably sell copper, no matter how low the world price goes. As with many other Chilean schemes, Chile's rainy-day fund has been copied by many countries, including seven US states.

In 1980, the Pinochet government introduced another major economic innovation. The country's pension system went from a defined benefits program to defined contributions. Singapore had adopted such a savings scheme to fund retirement in the mid-1950s. However, it wasn't replacing an already existing savings scheme, as Chile was. Since its inception, there have been many reforms. However, the underlying principle of defined contributions has remained the bedrock of its retirement scheme. Countless countries have copied Chile's program, not just in Latin America, but throughout the world, including even such advanced economies as Italy. Italy's defined contribution scheme will over time replace the defined benefits program still in place for older workers.

For economic historians, one issue posed by Chile's economic performance in the 1970s and 1980s is, could it have been done without an authoritarian regime?

Despite my fear of seeing armed soldiers everywhere, I still came away impressed with how the economy and government finance was functioning. I became an early believer in Chile's ability to develop. As time passed, I soon became accustomed to seeing armed soldiers on city streets throughout the world, including New York City and Washington, DC, but for different reasons.

Peru

My next stop was Lima, Peru. International goods were in short supply in most Latin American countries in the 1970's. Import controls along with strict capital controls meant that few luxury goods were available. You might think that is not such a big deal. However, middle class and upper-class people missed having some *vital* foreign items. Besides meeting with the central bank, the US Embassy, the IMF team, etc., I was going to meet with expatriate bankers who worked for one of Peru's largest banks. Before my arrival, they had asked me to buy them Scotch. I obliged. After meeting them, I understood why.

One was a British expat. The other was an American expat who had a thick Brooklyn accent, which you don't hear as often today. Both had lived in Lima for at least thirty years. They invited me to their *club*. It was in the center of Lima. Lima is in a quasi-desert. Despite the fact that it doesn't rain much, the sky is usually overcast and gray. Why on earth the Spanish made this their Vice-Regal capital is beyond my understanding. If they had chosen a spot a little further north, they could have lived in a bright and sunny place, instead of gloomy Lima. Given the shortage of water, there weren't many trees around. Most buildings were made of cement, stone or other similar materials as is often the case throughout Latin America. The big surprise on entering their club was to find that it looked like a British pub had just been dropped from the sky, landing in Peru. Everything was made of the finest woods. It looked like it was an outpost of the Empire.

The real fun began when my two banker colleagues began telling me how they viewed Peru. They could have been a comedy team. Their two accents couldn't have been more different. They did nothing but insult each other, yet it was obvious that the insults were simply good fun for them.

I quickly surmised they were trying to get me very drunk. Their bottles of Scotch were already put away. They were going to introduce me to real Peruvian life, first through food and more importantly through drink. I ate Peru's version of ceviche, a delicious fish meal, where the marinade *cooks* the fish. Then they introduced me to pisco sours. I was told how *superior* Peruvian pisco was to Chilean pisco. Both are made from grapes fermented to a high degree of alcohol. It reminded me of Italian grappa. It's a very strong drink, which doesn't seem potent because juices and sometimes even wines added to it, mask its wallop. Let's put it this way, they kept plying me with pisco sour after pisco sour. I had caught on to their plot, which I interpreted as wanting me to get so drunk that I would add to their levity. I didn't fall for it. I finally said, "No more drinks!"

The next day, I was taken by other bankers to their country club outside Lima. I was amazed to see the country club's verdant grass in desert-like Lima. I asked my hosts how it was maintained. They told me that once a week, the ground was flooded by water up to about one-foot deep. The water then settled in and kept the grass luxuriously green until the following week's watering. The class divide here was enormous.

Peru was ruled by a small European and Japanese elite. Most of the Peruvian population was either mestizo or made up of indigenous people. The population mix was quite different from Chile, which was predominantly European. In 1975, there was a bloodless coup in Peru, where one section of the Peruvian military overthrew another military dictator. Both government juntas were leftist. Nationalizations had occurred, and land reform had begun. The problem for Peruvian land reform was that there wasn't much arable land to begin with. Both military juntas also wasted vast sums of money buying arms from the Soviet Union. The Peruvians wanted to retake land from Chile, which Peru had lost in the War of the Pacific in 1879. I would learn that minor territorial disputes have plagued Latin America for centuries. From my perspective, the funds spent on weapons were simply a waste of vital foreign exchange. Some estimates of such spending by Peru were as high as $2 billion. Overall, Peru faced high inflation, a big international debt, and an unhappy elite who felt that their land was being confiscated without adequate compensation. Not surprisingly, Peru's politics would remain volatile and subject to more military interventions.

Ecuador

My next stop was Quito, Ecuador. Being about 8000 feet above sea level and near the equator, Quito was appropriately known as the City of Eternal Spring. Quito was pleasant to visit. Unlike Lima, Quito wasn't dangerous. Crime was low. As I learned over time, the higher the proportion of indigenous people, the lower the crime rate usually is. Guayaquil, Ecuador's port city, was mainly mestizo, and like Lima, it had a high crime rate. A statistical fact.

Oil was becoming more important to Ecuador since oil prices had quadrupled in 1973. The country had top notch people in its elite, and hard-working people, but without much education at the bottom. The one thing Ecuador lacked was a mid-level cadre of managers and supervisors.

Because of the city's high elevation, the main places for local vacationing were in the deep valleys. The deeper the valley, the higher the level of oxygen. One valley, in particular, was known as the ideal place to go on honeymoon. Easy to understand why.

In the future, I would become quite familiar with Ecuador's banana farms, as one of the wealthiest banana magnates regularly received economic presentations by me, when he and his wife visited New York.

Argentina

My next major trip to South America was to Argentina. Argentina proved to be one of the more fascinating places to visit. It had, and has, many idiosyncrasies. Let's begin with a few simple comments about Argentine history. In 1910, Argentina is estimated to have had the same per capita income as the US. After World War II, Argentina gave foreign aid to Europe. Despite a few glimmers of fleeting hope, it's been downhill ever since.

When I arrived in Argentina, I was surprised how different it was from other countries in Latin America I had already visited. Buenos Aires looked like a European city, but which was caught in a time warp, and dropped onto the eastern coast of South America. The architecture was Italianate. The boulevards were French. The language was Spanish but spoken with an Italian accent. The rhythm of the language was Italian, not Castilian. The population was almost exclusively of European origin, with Italians and Spanish making up the two largest groups.

The subway system copied European designs. Educational levels were as high as Europe. In the 1970s, Argentina had a higher percentage of university graduates than France. Yet, the country was endemically in financial crisis. When I was studying economic development, one of the text books claimed that if you wanted to study everything you shouldn't do to an economy, simply study Argentina and Libya. The course pre-dated the oil crisis, since Libya would look quite a bit better by the mid-1970s, at least economically.

Much of the blame for the worst economic detours dated from the Peronist period of 1946-1955. Some would argue that the huge welfare state created by Juan and Eva Peron was the culprit. I would argue it is far more complex. One major problem was the Argentine obsession with removing any signs of foreign influence. The government wasted great amounts of international political capital after World War II because it opposed US influence in an increasingly divided two-superpower world.

Since Peronism is, and was, a hodgepodge of economic and political beliefs, it has sometimes been dubbed as right-wing fascist, corporatist, left-wing socialist, just to name a few of the more usual descriptions. Impossible to pin down.

Needless to say, countless books and studies have been bemoaning Argentina's many woes. I don't need to go into them all here. The bottom line is that the turbulent economic and political reality of post-World War II Argentina made it truly unique among nations.

My first meetings with government officials were interesting. Phones didn't work, so every official had several phones on his desk. Every single meeting started late. The most memorable meeting took place in the central bank.

As I have already noted, I wasn't familiar with Charlotte before learning about NCNB. Therefore, it was no surprise that this central bank official didn't know anything about North Carolina. At first, we chatted about Argentine economic developments. Then, as so often has been the case around the world, I was asked about my ethnicity. He told me he surmised that I was of Italian origin by my name. Not too hard for an Argentinian. Then he asked me to describe North Carolina. I told him about the economy, including the breakdown into manufacturing and agriculture. I told him about the population, which I described as about 25-30 percent African-American, with most of the rest being White Anglo-Saxon Protestants. Then he got serious. He leaned across the desk as though we were about to discuss something, not just important, but worthy of only speaking about it in hushed tones. He asked, **"You must tell me. What is it like to live with Anglo-Saxons?"**

I was floored. At first, I didn't even know what to say. I then told him that I had never given it any thought. What his question told me was something that I would find proven time and time again: Argentines look at the world from a unique perspective. Always expect the unexpected.

When I mentioned that the next stop on my trip was Brazil, every Argentine gave me their impressions of Brazil, none of which were flattering. They considered Brazil less civilized than Argentina. There were quite a few comments about race, especially the fact that Brazil was far more racially mixed than Argentina. Since I had already visited Brazil as a grad student, I just listened.

My trip to Brazil was uneventful. I met with government officials and with businessmen in Rio and Sao Paolo.

Mexico

Al Smith and I together visited Mexico City. In the late 70s, Mexico was going through an unprecedented economic boom fueled by major oil discoveries and growing export earnings from oil. The Mexican economy historically performed like a roller coaster. High growth was quickly followed by a bust. In 1976, Mexico had to devalue the peso by about 60 percent. Then with oil income on the rise, and a profligate fiscal policy, the economy started growing rapidly once again. However, it was clear from the 1976 crisis that fiscal policy was mismanaged and corrupt to the core. Despite rapidly rising export revenue, the government managed to spend so much that more foreign borrowing was required. This was the economic environment Al Smith and I were dealing with in 1977-78.

Mexico City's traffic was the worst I had seen up to that time. The pollution was horrible. Government officials were haughty and would say very little that was relevant to the economy since such information was often considered a state secret. There were no detailed foreign debt numbers. It wasn't clear if the public sector debt would or should be included in the overall measure of government debt. Pemex, the Mexican oil monopoly, was king. Frankly, it was just hard to make out what the underlying situation was really like, except to know that it was disorderly and opaque. I just couldn't get a handle on the country's economic fundamentals. Although, the country was not a dictatorship, it was not a democracy. The formal name of the governing party, the PRI (Institutional Revolutionary Party), provides the best insight into how dysfunctional the government really was. Institutional revolution is an oxymoron.

Imagine how bizarre international finance had become: Foreign banks lent to governments without accurate data. That's what went on in the 1970s, and on a grand scale. Crazy credit practices always end badly, and in this case, it ended as a catastrophe for countless countries around the world. We were worried, but as with all banks, sometimes lending occurs even when risks were high. That is a trade-off senior management must make.

South Africa Under Apartheid

The next country I visited was South Africa, where NCNB was a major lender. Most senior bank executives did not appear troubled by apartheid. They had grown up for most of their life living with segregation. My observation was that segregation was not always viewed as something bad by them, even if it had, by then, become illegal.

NCNB had a South African representative office, manned by a South African. As a result, when I visited South Africa, I had incredible access to people.

Getting to South Africa at the time was not easy. There were no direct flights. Most African countries banned South African Airways from flying over them. You had to take a big detour to get to Johannesburg from New York. It required a stopover in Ilha do Sal, in the Cape Verde Islands. The stopover gave me an insight into your stereotypical African dictatorships; cult of personality, huge pictures of the President hanging everywhere, and corruption at every turn.

Arriving in Johannesburg was no surprise. It looked like any other large city, with tall buildings and urban sprawl. I soon learned how complicated this country was.

I met with many businessmen in Johannesburg. Most were of British origin. English was the dominant commercial language. I also met some Afrikaner businessmen. The Afrikaners were, by far, the friendlier of the two groups.

The fundamental issue for country risk analysis came down to international politics. Could South Africa thrive in the world while still under apartheid? In the late 1970s, there wasn't a straightforward answer.

South Africa had many friends, particularly in Europe, with Switzerland and Germany providing lots of support. The support was not from the governments, but from wealthy and powerful businessmen.

Strong support was also provided by Israel. There were SAA flights to Tel Aviv. They too had to make a big swoop to avoid flying over other African countries. The NCNB rep told me his father was a close friend of Menachem Begin, who had vacationed often in South Africa. Both South Africa and Israel had close military and economic ties that would last for decades. Another surprising fact for me was how friendly Iran was to South Africa. This was before the Iranian Revolution of 1979. The Shah's father, who had been sent into exile, lived in South Africa during that period. The Shah never forgot how South Africa had helped him and his family. The world is a complicated place.

After visiting Johannesburg, I was taken to Pretoria, the country's administrative capital. What I remember most about Pretoria were the jacaranda trees, which were in full bloom. They provided a glorious purple canopy in all directions. After meetings with government officials in Pretoria, I was taken to the Voortrekker Monument outside Pretoria. This was devoted to remembering the long trek Afrikaner forefathers had made beginning in the 1830s. These Afrikaners left the Cape Colony headed inland to avoid the British. It's an imposing monument, but what I remember most is the wall around the monument, which consists of a wagon train made up of sixty-four wagons in a closed circle, symbolizing the Trekkers efforts to keep out the Zulus.

I was told on countless occasions that the Zulus had only migrated into South Africa around the mid-1600s, or at about the same time as the Dutch and other Europeans arrived in the Cape. This was meant to indicate that there were two forces moving into the country at about the same time, differentiating it from other colonial adventures.

Today, this is obviously a controversial explanation of history, and more importantly, pre-history. What matters most, in this context, is that this was believed by most South African whites, Europeans and Americans at the time.

I had heard not only from Afrikaners, but from other whites as well, that the Afrikaners saw their role as fulfilling God's plan. They believed they were obligated *to civilize* the black population. I remember being told by our rep, who was not Afrikaans, that if a black person had a flat tire on the road, a white of British descent would simply drive by, while an Afrikaner would probably stop and help the black man. It would be his personal obligation.

I had fascinating meetings in Cape Town, the legislative capital of the country. The one that impressed me the most was my meeting with Helen Suzman. For many years, she was the most important anti-apartheid political leader in South Africa.

She was first elected to Parliament in 1952 as a member of the United Party. She and a group of other legislators split from the United Party and formed the Progressive Federal Party (PFP). Its main agenda was granting full civil rights to all South Africans, regardless of color. However, from 1961 until 1973, she was the sole PFP MP. It was Helen Suzman, standing alone in parliament, fighting against apartheid. In 1974, other like-minded MPs were elected, ending her legislative isolation.

She opposed apartheid but was against international sanctions against South Africa. She argued that sanctions would hurt blacks far more than whites. No wonder a meeting with her was viewed as essential. She provided the only rational argument I had heard against sanctions.

When visiting Cape Town, I was taken to Cape Point. It was amazing. It is a point where the warm blue Indian Ocean meets the cold, green South Atlantic. The technical point marking the divide between the Atlantic and the Indian Ocean is further to the east, but oceanic differences can migrate depending on oceanic and weather conditions. Anyway, who cares? It was breathtaking and is one of the most beautiful places on earth.

I was also taken north of Cape Town to Stellenbosch, where a famous Afrikaans-language university was located. I say "was" because Afrikaans is slowly being replaced by English as a teaching language in the university, much to the dismay of Afrikaners.

The surrounding region is the heart of South Africa's wine country. We toured vineyards and wineries, with tastings along the way. I was already familiar with South African wines, sherries and ports. I knew they were good value for the money.

At one of the wineries, I met a man who told me he was a direct descendent of Henry Hudson. Another wow! Here I was meeting a direct descendent of the man who *discovered* New York for the Dutch in the early 1600s, yet we were now nearly four centuries later, and about 8000 miles away New York.

As a special treat, I was given a taste of what they said was their most magnificent port. It dated from 1929. It was superb! It was smooth, but also incredibly complex. I wouldn't have minded spending more time in Stellenbosch.

When back in Johannesburg, the NCNB rep took me to Soweto, which at the time was off-limits for most whites. I was surprised to see that it was not simply one enormous slum. There were nice neighborhoods and there were shacks. It wasn't very different, on the surface, from many places I had already seen in EM countries. There was one enormous difference; the people living there had no right to live in white areas. They weren't even allowed to stay overnight in Johannesburg. I kept thinking to myself, how was this all going to end?

From South Africa, I flew to Rome, with a stop in Zaire. At the Kinshasa airport, I saw several planes that were being hidden from foreign creditors who were trying to repossess them to collect on loans gone sour. Air Zaire had to be careful not to fly these planes to countries where a US or UK judgment would be respected. That was par for the course in Zaire.

What most amazed me about this trip from Johannesburg to Rome was how huge Africa was. I believe the flight lasted about 11 hours. It would not be the last time I would visit sub-Sahara Africa.

Life in the South

Over the two years I worked at NCNB, I traveled to more countries, and slowly built up the files necessary for doing the economic and political analysis required. During this time, my parents came to visit me in Charlotte. They both thought that it was a beautiful place to live. To my surprise, my father said that if he was younger, he would have moved there. Other family members regularly visited me, and all of them liked Charlotte, and its comfortable lifestyle. I must remind you that this was in the 1970s, well before Charlotte really expanded.

Life in the South at that time was a bit strange for me. The first jarring thing was the significance of Bible Belt religion. Life outside work centered around church. Even in religiously zealous Ireland, while attending church was important at the time, social life centered around the pub, not the church. In Charlotte, on Sunday morning, there was almost nothing on TV, but religious programs. That's when I saw my first televangelists. Life slowed down noticeably on Sundays. I got used to it. It reminded me of Sundays in New York and New Jersey before all the *blue laws* disappeared.

Another difference was the summer. In New York City, never mind Montreal, you would get very hot and humid days, sometimes lasting for several weeks. However, they were always followed by cool breaks, with temperatures maxing out in the upper 70sF. In Charlotte, it was different. It began to get hot in late May and remained hot through September. Temperatures in the 90s were normal, with high humidity. I loved it. Hot weather never bothered me. I could go swimming almost any day if I wished at my apartment complex's pool. I did have to make one heat-related adjustment, and that was I needed to buy a new car.

The car I was driving had no air conditioning and a black interior, definitely not the best choice for living in Charlotte. I remember bringing my car to have a minor repair. When the mechanic lifted the car, he said to me, "This car came from the North." When I asked how he knew, he said it was obvious. Corrosion underneath caused by salt on the roads made it a no-brainer.

Another big difference was the treatment of alcohol. Everywhere I had ever been didn't make a big fuss over alcohol, except in Ireland which I have already talked about. North Carolina was not totally dry when I arrived, but restrictions on drinking were strict. The state allowed government-owned Alcohol Beverage Control (ABC) stores to operate in counties or cities where the local people had approved it. Mecklenburg County, where Charlotte is located, allowed beer and wine sales in restaurants. However, *liquor-by-the-drink* wasn't allowed until 1978. It was Charlotte's main political issue during my stay there.

It may seem odd, but the issue centered around divergent views of where the South should be headed. Those who opposed alcohol sales viewed it as a kind of poison, causing all sorts of societal ills. They were deeply religious evangelicals who wanted to avoid turning their region into carbon copies of Northern urban areas, which they detested as decadent.

Those supporting liquor sales wanted the region to develop rapidly. One of the first ways would be to entice businesses and tourists to visit. Liquor sales were an important way to do that. Until 1978, the only way you could have hard liquor of any kind in a restaurant was to bring it in a brown paper bag. Then you had to pour the drink while holding the bottle under the table. It was outright embarrassing for local businessmen to be entertaining businessmen from other states, and increasingly from other countries.

Also, they looked forward to revitalizing the traditional center of Charlotte, called oddly enough, Uptown. When I arrived, it was pretty deserted and looked just like any other city center that had been hollowed out by suburban malls. Except for the big bank buildings, the area appeared pretty desolate, especially at night, when it became a center for the usual criminal activities you would expect.

One person, Hugh McColl, who I knew quite well at the time, was President of NCNB. He told me and others about how the bank was going to turn around the area by restoring some of the old buildings and building upscale urban housing there, which would revitalize nightlife.

When I left Charlotte, there were already early signs that it was going to happen.

I can't leave out describing Hugh McColl more. You have to remember that NCNB was a small institution. It wouldn't have been strange to have Mr. McColl come down to the employee cafeteria and join others at their lunch tables. He was fascinating. He was a short, wiry ex-marine. He was totally no-nonsense. He was also ambitious beyond anyone I have met before or since.

I don't think he trusted Northerners. Everyone, and I mean everyone, who worked for the bank, almost without exception, had strong southern accents. That meant my, by-now, flat Mid-Atlantic accent stood out. McColl surely felt I was an outsider, but there must have something he liked, because he and Jim Sommers used to joke with me that they would eventually make me into a proper Southern gentleman. I'm not sure what that meant, but I took it as a compliment.

McColl had a vision of NCNB becoming the largest bank throughout the South, spreading all the way to California. This was an unbelievable vision, because you need to remember that interstate banking was not permitted at the time. That didn't stop him from preparing the way through various deals NCNB had already made in Florida and California, which eventually led NCNB to become the first bank to cross state lines.

I always thought that I would eventually move back to New York to be nearer to my family. I was at a point in life where if I settled down, I was likely to stay for a long time. After much soul-searching, I realized that if I didn't go back to New York soon, I would probably stay in Charlotte for *the duration*. It was a tough decision, but I decided to try to get a job in New York.

Mr. Cordell, the man who found me my job at NCNB, had one rule he never violated. He would never contact someone he had placed. It just wasn't ethical. He said that former clients could contact him. That was their choice.

I decided to give Mr. Cordell a phone call. Once again, I was surprised to hear that he had just been contacted by Irving Trust. They were looking for someone to add to their economics department, specializing in country risk analysis. Another Wow moment! This was early September 1979. Since I now had experience, despite my young age, I was a viable candidate. If I hadn't gotten the job at NCNB, even if I found a position at a New York bank, it would have been only menial in nature.

I went to New York to interview at Irving Trust. I was soon offered a job along with the title of Assistant Vice President. The offer included a pay rise of about 50 percent. I decided it was time to return home.

When I told my colleagues at NCNB, Al Smith understood. He thought it was a good career move, as well as understanding why I wanted to return to New York. After all, he had studied at Columbia, yet he still returned home to the Carolinas.

Jim Sommers had a different reaction. He didn't want me to leave. I explained for the second or third time that I wished to return to New York because my family was there. It was absolutely not a reflection on my job at NCNB or of Charlotte. His response caught me off guard. He said that NCNB would be willing to pay for weekend flights twice a month to New York. I was not just flattered, I found it very tempting. Although I knew my pay would go up by about 50 percent if I joined Irving Trust, with New York City and State income taxes, along with a much higher cost of living, it really wouldn't be much of a raise. I had to give serious thought to his innovative offer.

The flight between New York and Charlotte was about 90 minutes. Then there was the hassle of going to and from airports. Still, it was certainly doable. In addition, since he thought so well of me, I was likely to rise through the ranks of NCNB. When I told Al Smith about the offer, he understood my dilemma. He said that such an arrangement was certainly doable over the short-term, but I should ask myself if I would be willing to do that over many years. Al was right. It would be too exhausting. I thanked Jim Sommers, but regrettably told him I was still leaving. I never imagined leaving one job for another would be so difficult. Another part of growing up.

Irving Trust

Irving Trust paid for my move to New York. My Aunt Christine came down to help me with the move. I had a small one-bedroom apartment. However, it was revealing for me to see the movers were able to pack up all my things in just a few short hours and move them out to the truck. By midday, there was no sign I had ever lived there. It was an odd feeling.

When I got to New York, I immediately found an apartment close to where my parents lived. Since Irving Trust's main headquarters was located at One Wall Street, and since I now lived in southern Westchester County, my commute was terrible and long. My apartment was nothing like the bright and cheery place I had in Charlotte with its swimming pool and tennis courts. Moving back to New York made my life much more difficult.

Also, it turned out that my first boss, Gordon Pye, was an unusual man and not in a good way. After finding an apartment, I needed to have my belongings moved out of storage.

I had grown accustomed to Southern civility. My colleagues and bosses had been a pleasure to work with. However, when I asked Mr. Pye if I could have a day off to be home when the movers came, he said, "No." I was floored. It wasn't like I was asking for something completely out of line. I kept thinking that maybe I had made a big mistake leaving NCNB. Fortunately, my mother and aunt were there for the move.

Irving Trust was one of the oldest banks in the country. Although it was only about 13th in size, at the time, it was the second largest correspondent bank in the country. That meant that Irving Trust was a bank for other banks, both domestically and especially internationally. As I would eventually learn, all international dollar transactions, no matter where they are made, are always mirrored by transactions in New York. The only exception is when transactions are in dollar bills.

I must admit I didn't learn this on day one at Irving Trust, nor in any economic course, nor in any academic article. Rather, over the years, I would learn banking from some of the best and most knowledgeable bankers I've ever met.

The Economics Department totaled about 20 people, with some being dedicated to domestic economics and the others involved in international economics. It was a pretty impressive and knowledgeable group.

It took me a while to adjust to the kind of reports that were required at Irving Trust. But I did after a few weeks. Mr. Pye still did not create a pleasant work environment. It took years before he became easier to deal with.

The international economists were not organized by region. We each had an eclectic group of countries to work on. The bank had country ceilings, or a limit on how much exposure the bank would allow in any country. These limits were decided by a credit committee composed of the main economist for the country, the lead bank officer responsible for that country, various senior credit officers, and the Senior Credit Officer. It was here that I truly learned country risk analysis. I began to understand the close relationship between specific financial transactions and risk. As time passed, I was eventually asked to sit on countless credit committees involving important banks and companies located in countries, which by now, I knew well. I would speak about the economics and politics, but I learned so much more from the bankers about the nitty-gritty of doing business in those places. Doing business in emerging markets required a good deal of knowledge about the political environment, which successful bankers needed to master. It was definitely a joint effort.

After arriving at Irving Trust, I soon began to resume my intense travel schedule, which lasted for decades. I would have the same complications traveling for Irving Trust, compared to my travel at NCNB, except that it would involve many more countries in many more diverse parts of the world.

The West Coast of South America (Again)

One of my first trips was to the West Coast of South America. That was fortunate because I had already worked on those countries.

In Chile, it seemed that the economy was continuing to develop in a healthy manner. The expansion, which started after the 1975 recession, continued. Chileans had also just approved a new constitution. Not surprisingly, Pinochet won.

On the other hand, Peru was in a worse mess because a brutal civil war broke out between the government and Maoist guerrillas, under the banner of Sendero Luminoso or Shining Path. The civil war would last for decades, involving the death of over 70,000 people. The military dictatorship ended in 1980, when Peruvians elected a former president, Fernando Belaunde, who had been ousted by a military in a coup in 1968. Despite witnessing the beginning of a civil war, the Peruvian government went to war with neighboring Ecuador over some minor border outposts in the Cordillera del Condór. It was a territorial dispute dating to 1840, with the most recent war having occurred in 1941. The main impact of this unnecessary war was that both countries would now spend much more on the military, leaving less for economic development. The Peruvians also still wanted to retake their territory lost to Chile in the 19th century, causing still more money to be wasted.

Ecuador, too, was in worse economic shape. The main culprit was the slowly declining price of oil, now the country's largest export earner. In addition, political discourse was becoming radicalized among the conservatives, leftists and the extreme left. It would not make dealing with the country's growing economic crisis easier to handle. Fistfights and throwing chairs became routine in the country's legislature.

Travel and Disease

What I remember most about my trip to Ecuador was that when I returned, I got increasingly sick. I began to run a low-grade fever. I felt like I had a flu, but it was definitely not flu. I had absolutely no energy. I tried to keep going to work because I knew how difficult Mr. Pye would be. Nonetheless, as the days passed, I became increasingly weak. When I went to the doctor, he said that my liver functions were off by about 400 percent. I had no idea what that actually meant, except that I was very, very sick. He gave me antibiotics, but he didn't think they would work because he said I had viremia, in other words, a virus that couldn't be identified.

Looking back, I'm not sure why my doctor didn't send me to the hospital, but he didn't. My parents and Aunt Christine came to stay with me. I felt so sick that I genuinely didn't care if I died. I just wanted the illness and discomfort to end. It was this experience that would allow me to empathize later with people who feel so sick that they would just prefer to die. It was a frightening realization.

What happened next was incredible. I got sicker, but this time my temperature suddenly went up to about 104F. My throat suddenly got very sore. This time, the doctor prescribed antibiotics to deal with my very sore throat. Then, almost miraculously, I started to feel much better. In just a few days, I felt fine. When the doctor tested my liver functions again, they had come back to near normal. He surmised that my bacterial infection, which affected my throat, was so bad that it pushed up my fever to a level which killed the virus. He said viruses don't tolerate high temperatures. No matter, I was cured, and ready to go back to work.

I have no idea how I got viremia. I had followed all normal precautions about what food and liquids to consume. I hadn't had any close bodily contact with anyone during my travels. It just happened. Following this episode, I became *a regular* at the Cornell Tropical Disease Clinic in Manhattan. I believe today it's called the Infectious Disease Center.

Besides getting the latest medicines to deal with diarrhea, I also learned to get gamma-globulin shots before going on *exotic* trips. At a time before there were vaccines against the various strains of hepatitis, gamma-globulin was considered a good prophylactic. The doses were really big. The nurse had to massage the medicine in after giving the injection. Also, it didn't provide protection for a long period of time. After going through what I had just gone through, I had no qualms about getting it whenever necessary.

Over the years, I would return to the Cornell clinic, but for different reasons, none of which ever came close to my viremia experience.

The Falklands/Malvinas War: Its Impact

Since these west coast countries were important for Irving Trust, I regularly visited them. As oil prices kept declining, and the Mexican economy was overheating, a geopolitical event in the South Atlantic would have serious consequences and become an indirect trigger for events in the summer of 1982.

The source of the problem was Argentina. The military junta faced severe criticism at home and abroad for the brutal treatment of political dissidents. As usual, the Argentine economy was also under enormous stress. It was still reeling from the 1976 economic and political crisis caused by the presidency of Juan Peron's second wife, Isabella. Towards the end of her presidency, inflation soared to triple digit levels. Such rates of inflation represent a demonetization of the economy. The nominal money supply rises, but the real money supply collapses. Not surprisingly, the military staged another coup. The military junta was brutal in its treatment of dissidents. Beyond brutality, the military government proved as inept as the Peronist government they replaced. They continued their foreign borrowing binge.

With warning signs of problems, which were being seen across the EM world, the junta decided to do one of the dumber things it could possibly do, and that was to invade the Falkland Islands, known as the Malvinas in Argentina. I argue it was dumb because here was a small country, already in financial and political crisis, taking on the UK. There was no way they could win. Most observers believed it was done to unite Argentines in an Argentine version of a Great Patriotic War – this was obviously not similar in any way to the Russians fighting the Nazis. It was just traditional Argentine bluster at its worst.

The Falklands were claimed by several world powers over the centuries. In 1833, the British occupied the islands, once again, and stayed there ever since. The only possible explanation for the invasion by Argentina was that they imagined Britain wouldn't fight over these distant, and at the time, poor outposts in the South Atlantic (there was growing talk about hydrocarbons off the Falklands, but this was still speculation in 1982). The Argentines had no idea that the British Prime Minister, Margaret Thatcher, was not a pushover.

The predecessor of the EU, the European Economic Community (EEC) placed stiff sanctions on Argentina. The US sided with the UK. Even Chile sided with the UK because Chile and Argentina had been having a dispute over the Beagle Channel, at the tip of South America. Eventually, the Beagle Channel dispute would be resolved by the Vatican, but that was years in the future.

The result of the war was a foregone conclusion. The British recaptured the Falklands. Argentines were furious with the stupidity of the military junta, which they quickly ousted. Democracy returned to the country and has been maintained ever since.

Despite this, Argentina has suffered economic and political crises on a regular basis. As a borrower, the Argentine government is a *serial defaulter*.

During one of the county's many attempts to reform radically, in the mid-1990s, it adopted a modified version of a currency board. Currency boards have worked quite well in many places around the world, most notably in Hong Kong. The system was also used successfully in Singapore for many years. Several British possessions, such as the Cayman Islands, Bermuda and the East Caribbean islands, use the dollar as central to their system. Gibraltar and the Falklands use the British pound as their anchor. Currency boards have also been used on occasion in Eastern Europe.

Well-functioning currency boards must meet four basic requirements: 1) the economy must be small; 2) domestic prices must be flexible; 3) the external sector must be large compared to the domestic economy; and, 4) the government must have low debt.

The problem was that Argentina met none of these requirements. On top of that, instead of strongly anchoring its peso to the US dollar, allowing everything else to adjust to the availability of dollars, Argentina allowed for the creation of peso liquidity that surpassed the amount of dollars in the economy. In other words, disaster was guaranteed.

The problem was that initially the system seemed to work. The economic and financial dislocations would not be obvious for several years. Then as government debt denominated in dollars and pesos grew, the overall system was plunging toward crisis.

I don't think anything has been published about how J.P. Morgan-Chase tried to help Argentina avoid defaulting in 2001. Avoiding default would have given the government more time to try to fix the system or abandon it in a more orderly fashion.

Moody's provided a service, which would not be permitted today by new regulations (another example of dumb regulations). As Managing Director responsible for Latin America within the Moody's Sovereign Risk Unit, I was approached by the bank to provide an indicative rating given different scenarios. It was similar to what structured finance does on a regular basis. One hard and fast rule was that the rating agency could not provide scenarios, but only react to scenarios presented by the bank. Since the bank wasn't the issuer, we required the bank to get permission from the Argentine government to allow them to undertake this project. The government did.

Any indicative rating for a scenario was presented to a formal rating committee, voting on what rating a scenario would receive if all the terms of the scenario were met. It took time for the bankers to come up with various scenarios. Eventually, they provided us with a scenario, which went brought to a sovereign rating committee resulted in a Ba2 rating for the new bonds. Given that Argentine government bonds were in the B3-Caa range, this would have represented a huge improvement in the rating, and a dramatic drop in default risk, making restructuring under the terms of the scenario relatively easy.

What happened next shocked me and the bankers. The Argentine government rejected the proposal. Soon after, the government defaulted on its debt in one of the world's worst default crises. Not only did it default on its peso and dollar-denominated debt, but it allowed the peso to float, froze bank accounts, and caused a complete collapse of the banking system. People were limited to small peso withdrawals from ATMs. The economy was in a free fall.

Eventually, as with all things, the crisis abated, but not for several years and at huge human cost. I still think about what might have happened if the government had accepted the J.P. Morgan proposal. The result might have proved very different.

Months before, the Argentine Finance Minister demanded to meet with Moody's Chairman, John Rutherfurd. He was going to express Argentine outrage at Moody's low rating for the country. The meeting was memorable. We all sat around a large table with Mr. Rutherfurd sitting across from the Finance Minister. When the Minister started to complain to him, John interrupted him and said, "When you are sick and, in a hospital, and need to discuss your medical treatment, you speak to your doctors, not to the hospital administrator. I'm the hospital administrator. Mr. Truglia and his team are the doctors." That ended that debate.

When the Falklands War was underway, I was visiting Chile. An important Irving Trust client was a steel manufacturer. The chairman invited me to fly down to see their steel mill, which was located in Concepcion, a city about 270 miles south of Santiago. I always liked to tour factories, so I accepted. I was staying at the CEO's country home.

I had never been in a steel mill before. It was fascinating. For the first time, I realized how dangerous steel manufacturing could be. Huge vats of molten steel high overhead gave off tremendous blasts of heat.

The topography of Concepcion is quite different from Santiago. Santiago is surrounded by the Andes on the east and by the Coastal Range on the west. It was breathtaking on the few days when the mountains weren't out of sight because of dense smog. Concepcion is along the coast. To the east, the mountains between Chile and Argentina are not very high. They looked more like the Poconos or the Catskill mountains.

While there, we got word that the British were beginning to retake the islands. Since I knew Chile had sided with the British and not the Argentines, I asked my host how far we were from the Argentina border. His response, "About 4 hours by tank." That said it all.

Once again, I made my way north, stopping off in Lima. I was sitting in the office of the head of debt management. His desk was topped by several phones. I sat there quietly, as he was getting very upset with the phone calls. After several calls, he told me that he had been spending all day trying to convince London-based banks that Peru was not physically close to Argentina. He said he actually had to emphasize that his country was on the west coast, not the east coast of South America. He then told me that access to funds was suddenly getting more difficult for Peru. His argument was that it was becoming irrational. More groundwork was being laid for the coming global crisis.

I worked for Irving Trust for thirteen years, but since I didn't keep notes on my travels, I really can't remember, after the first months at the bank, which trip occurred when. The exceptions are those trips associated with events that are easily dated, such as the Falklands War. Going forward, in many cases, I will be forced to write about events in broader non-chronological terms.

Economic Briefings

Irving Trust's economics department had a Chart Room, which at the time, was considered a marvel. At a time before computers became ubiquitous, making charts with graphs and bars was tedious. Making them large enough to put in front of an audience required a lot of labor. We had three people who did nothing but produce 2' X 3' charts, which were displayed on a series of felt boards in the chart room. This allowed for updating data as it was published.

The economists were obliged, on a regular basis, to give presentations on economic conditions to the staff. In addition, we gave presentations to important bank customers. That necessitated each of us to keep track of what was happening overall in the US and the rest of the world.

We each traveled around the US giving customer briefings to varied audiences. Doing these presentations in places I would never have visited otherwise, I learned lots about middle America. Visiting the Midwest was fascinating. Long drives between locations provided a glimpse of a country I apparently knew little about. It was great.

Since we were always accompanied by someone from client services on these trips, I always had company on these trips. One question I raised on my trips with my colleagues who did the driving, but to which I never got a satisfactory answer was, "Why are all barns painted red?"

I heard a myriad of theories, which I thoroughly enjoyed hearing.

It didn't take long to see that there was a big difference between the Northeast, the South and the Midwest. What stood out most was that Midwesterners seemed friendly, but in a way quite different from the South. Sometimes Southern hospitality was superficial. Midwestern friendliness always seemed genuine, with the one exception being Minnesota, which I was always warned not to be fooled by *Minnesota niceness*!

Mexico: Ground Zero for the 1980s Debt Crisis

Traveling around the US giving briefings to large corporations unexpectantly turned out to be quite helpful in doing country risk analysis. On one trip, I met with the senior management of a GM company responsible for making locomotives. After talking about the US and world economy, we then talked about their business. I learned that Mexico's railways were so inefficient that they couldn't keep track of where locomotives were at any given time. Whole trains seemed to vanish in the overall chaos. The economy was so overheated that trains were backed up 500 miles into Texas waiting to enter Mexico. Box cars were often used as storage containers. The most shocking point I learned was that since the Mexicans couldn't find their locomotives, which were somewhere in Mexico, they simply bought new ones from this GM company. It was definitely good for GM, but indicative of how screwed up the Mexican economy had become. This was the first blinking yellow light that a crisis in Mexico was approaching, but I doubt anyone knew the extent of the trauma that would result from what happened on August 15, 1982.

That day was hot and humid in New York – no surprise there. Marty Stern, Irving Trust's senior credit officer, was invited to attend a meeting at the New York Fed. The Mexican government was going to make a presentation. The world changed that afternoon. It was announced that Mexico was defaulting on its foreign currency loans. A moratorium would be put into place and the peso was devalued. The impact of this announcement would be felt for decades, affecting not just other EM countries, but also major banks and other financial institutions.

How did Mexico get to this point? As noted above, the Mexican economy was obviously overheated. At the same time, oil prices had been declining for several years. Since there was no public information on Mexican government borrowing, it was not clear how much the country needed to borrow on a regular basis to stay afloat. We learned, only by word of mouth, that they needed at least $1 billion per week. A problem with one loan being arranged was the government was arguing over the so-called spread over LIBOR (London Interbank Offering Rate), the benchmark price for international loans. The Mexicans wouldn't budge, and creditors wouldn't give in. The loan was delayed. Such a delay made refinancing other loans coming due, all the more difficult. I would argue that this was the immediate cause that triggered the default. If only the government had given in a bit by a few basis points, the default might have been avoided or at least delayed. Such a tiny sum of money caused a human catastrophe in many EM countries, having nothing to do with Mexico.

Within a relatively short period of time, sixteen Latin American countries would default. In addition, another eleven EM countries outside Latin America also defaulted.

A deeper explanation of country risk analysis will have to wait. It deserves a separate book.

It wasn't only countries which defaulted that were affected. The big banks were all heavily involved in EM lending, to a tune of multiples of their capital. The entire financial system was now at risk. It was such a big problem that governments in the creditor nations quickly got involved. Now, instead of simply trying to assess the risk of default, country risk analysis had to center on how the defaults would be resolved.

Despite the debt crisis, Irving Trust remained an important correspondent bank for many countries, which hadn't defaulted, especially in Eastern Europe and the Middle East.

I never traveled to Iran. However, the Iranian Revolution was a gamechanger for the Middle East. The Shah of Iran, a close US ally, was overthrown in February 1979. The speed of the revolution took everyone by surprise. I was still working for NCNB. Then I began to look at what warning signs I should have noticed but didn't. One of the most important proved to be on-going protests across Iran aimed at Bank Saderat. It turned out that Bank Saderat was a Beha'i-owned bank. I had never heard of Baha'is. I soon learned it was a religious minority that is viewed as heretical by most Muslims. Therefore, an attack against a persecuted religious minority should have warned me of the danger a Khomeini overthrow of the Shah would pose. It would be a theocratic revolution, the likes of which we hadn't seen for centuries.

As 1979 passed, tensions between Iran and the US grew. The Iranian hostage crisis began shortly after I started working at Irving Trust. The excuse given by the Iranians was that the US, following the Shah's overthrow, permitted the Shah to enter the US to receive medical treatment for cancer. The Shiite government didn't accept that the Shah would be allowed into the US because they held him accountable for human rights violations during his long reign. Our help for the Shah was considered proof of US complicity in the Shah's abuses. The Revolutionary Guard invaded the US embassy in Tehran and took 52 US hostages. The standoff would last for 444 days.

Iraq, under the leadership of Saddam Hussein, saw a theocratic Iran as a threat to his regime. In September 1980, Iraq invaded Iran. A long, bloody war would continue for eight years. Both countries would be sapped of their strength. Since Iran was viewed as a danger by the Western powers, most Westerners rooted for Iraq. The loss of lives on both sides was horrible. However, despite the war, Iraq remained prosperous. Iran was, by far, the bigger loser. Nonetheless, since the war ended in a stalemate, over time, Iran would prevail.

In the 1980s, despite being at war with Iran, Iraq had a thriving economy fueled by rising oil exports. It was growing so fast that it attracted about a million people from other Arab countries, especially from Egypt. Bank Rafidain, the country's largest bank, was known throughout the Middle East. They issued traveler's checks, which were as ubiquitous in the Middle East as American Express traveler's checks were around the world. The dollar-denominated checks indicated that they were payable at Irving Trust, One Wall Street. That added to the panache of the checks as well as provided a sense of security for users of those checks. For younger readers who may not be familiar with traveler's checks, I should explain that before credit and debit cards became ubiquitous, when you traveled, you needed cash. For security, people bought these traveler's checks for a one percent fee. They would countersign every time they wanted to use the checks. The great benefit was that if lost or stolen anywhere in the world, the checks could be easily replaced.

Although Saddam Hussein couldn't beat the Iranians, he held them at bay. He knew the only way to deal with a theocratic Shiite regime in Iran, was to increase his country's wealth and the size of the country's population, especially of Sunni Arabs.

In the 1980s, most westerners were just learning about the difference between Sunnis and Shiites. No one had really cared about the details of Islam, except as an intellectual curiosity. In Europe, only tiny Albania and a portion of Bosnia had significant Muslim communities. There were Muslims living in Germany (Turks), France (North Africans) and the UK (Pakistanis) and the Netherlands (Indonesians), but they were generally viewed as just another immigrant group.

If Hussein could expand Iraq into Sunni lands, that would aid him in his quest for Middle East hegemony. For geographical and historical reasons, Kuwait was the obvious first target.

All the Persian Gulf emirates were artificial creations of the British. They had no real historical significance before the discovery of massive amounts of oil. Before oil, they earned their living as traders or pearl fishermen. In contrast, Baghdad, Iraq's capital, was a major center of Arab culture, representing one of the pinnacles of Arab civilization. I am sure that deep down Hussein believed the Kuwaitis would be grateful if they united with Iraq. It would be a cultural step up in the world. Obviously, the Kuwaitis disagreed.

During the 1980s, I didn't visit Iraq. First, it was a war zone. Second, the bankers said it was so rich that a default seemed out of the question. Other nearby countries would keep me busy enough.

Turkey

On my first trip to Turkey in the early 1980s, what I heard, time and again from bankers, economists, embassy officials and academics, was how terrible things were before the 1980 military coup. Prior to the coup, a violent low-level civil war raged, pitting leftists against rightists. The biggest problem during the pre-coup period was that no one knew which side individual policemen were on. Some policemen supported the rightists, some supported the leftists. This made it risky to call for help. Calling for help might make matters worse.

Bankers told me they had to alternate which door they used to exit their bank buildings, as well as change their route home every day to avoid being attacked. Such stories reminded me of what I had heard years earlier from Chileans discussing the pre-Pinochet years.

As fighting continued unabated in the late 1970s, there was growing chorus calling for the Turkish military to intervene and end the fighting. According to all sources, with great reluctance, the military intervened in September 1980. To a person, the one complaint I heard from Turks during my early trips to Istanbul and Ankara was, "Why did the military wait so long before intervening?" No one appeared upset by the fact that a coup had occurred, even years after the coup when democracy had been restored. In their minds, things were better post-1980 coup.

Turgut Ozal played an important role throughout the period, and beyond. After the coup, Ozal was named Deputy Prime Minister. Prior to the 1980 military coup, he had become well-known for his emphasis on the need for economic reform. After disagreeing with the government over economic policy, he resigned and established a new political party in 1983, the Motherland Party, which won the next national election in late 1983. As leader of the party, Ozal became Prime Minister. His party would retain a majority in parliament until 1991.

No one indicated to me that the pre-coup fighting had anything to do with religion. However, I did hear often in the 80s that Ozal, a devout Muslim, was slowly beginning to spread Islam into government offices by introducing prayer rooms and other Islamic symbols. Although secularists were pleased by the stability of the government under Ozal, they indicated to me that this was a potentially dangerous development, which could threaten the secular state established by Ataturk in the 1920s. Otherwise, there was little reason to point out Ozal's religious devotion. I was also told that his wife wore a traditional headscarf, which they considered unacceptable.

My overall conclusion was that Turkey was a reasonable, short-term credit risk, but given its political history and tangled international alliances, I remained skeptical about its medium-term prospects. Since Irving Trust's main interest in Turkey lay in correspondent banking, our risks were overwhelmingly short-term.

I was struck by the vibrancy of Istanbul, a modern Middle Eastern version of a European metropolis. I still vividly remember watching dancing bears perform on the street.

During the 1980s, Russians (Soviets) and other Eastern Europeans were becoming important importers of Turkish goods. The Turkish businessmen I met would smile as they told me Turkey had many Soviet and Balkan *tourists*. Everyone knew these tourists were in Turkey solely to buy Western-style goods and then smuggle them back into their home countries. This contraband trade resulted in enormous profit. Turkey's land connection to Bulgaria and to the Caucasus republics of Armenia and Georgia was ideal for such trade. With a short-trip through Iran, these traders could also reach Azerbaijan.

Turkey was a master of pragmatic international politics. It's no wonder *Byzantine* is associated with all things complicated. It was a member of NATO, while its main enemy was Greece, another NATO member. Despite nominal support for the Palestinian cause, it had diplomatic relations with Israel. There were non-stop flights between Istanbul and Tel Aviv. At the same time, it secretly helped Iran export oil, which contravened international sanctions. It provided the Soviet Union with cheap versions of Western goods. Making money, at that time, lay at the heart of Turkish society.

In the 1980s, most women in Istanbul and Ankara wore western-style clothing. Some wore headscarves, but they were a small minority.

In the early years, I always stayed at the Istanbul Hilton. There weren't many five-star hotels in Istanbul. Over the years, that would change drastically. I still remember arriving in my room. When I walked to the outdoor balcony, the view was stunning. I was high above the Bosporus, the waterway connecting the Black Sea to the Mediterranean. This narrow strip of water separated Europe from Asia. I was in awe of the history this view represented. Istanbul was definitely worth a city tour.

After Istanbul, I always went to Ankara, the country's capital. It was totally different from Istanbul. It was in central Anatolia, Turkey's heartland. It was a small city with the usual boring architecture you would expect in a relatively new capital. The main attraction was Ataturk's Tomb, an imposing memorial to modern Turkey's founder. He created a secular state, and turned the former Ottoman heartland westwards, a Turkish version of Russia's Peter-the-Great.

Ataturk was revered. His picture was in every single office I visited, not just in government offices. The portrait always seemed the same. If there were variations, I never noticed them. What struck me was how these portraits made him look like Bela Lugosi's Dracula. More likely, Bela Lugosi copied Ataturk's look. I never dared say that to anyone. I felt it would be too disrespectful. Knowing his importance to modern Turkish history, I felt guilty even thinking that, but thought that I did.

Ankara lays in a basin, with hills all around it, similar to Los Angeles or Mexico City. It had horrible pollution. The smog was not only visible, you could smell it. It was very different from the pleasant smell of burning wood I remembered so fondly from winters in Perugia. This smell was industrial. One man who worked at the US embassy told me that whenever he left Ankara, he made sure to have his clothes dry cleaned to get rid of the smell. He warned me I would have to do the same. He was right. Rents increased the higher up the hills you lived, as the pollution diminished with altitude.

The pollution was caused by a dangerous mixture of car exhausts and fumes from burning coal, which was used to heat homes. Turkey was in the early stages of importing Russian natural gas, which eventually reduced the smog considerably. In later visits, I no longer needed to dry clean my clothes every time I left Ankara.

When back in Istanbul, on my first trip, I had time over a weekend to take my city tour. It was well worth it. The iconic Hagia Sofia is a world architectural masterpiece. Originally built as the main Orthodox Christian Cathedral in 537 A.D., it is breathtaking seen from both near and far. After the Ottoman conquest in the 15th century, it was turned into a mosque. Now it is a museum. When you walk inside, the interior of the dome is awe inspiring. It's hard to believe how such a magnificent building could have been built so long ago. When it was turned into a mosque, much of the original Christian artwork was either covered or destroyed. I would have to go to another smaller church to get an idea of what might have been seen in the original interior. Fortunately, in that church, the art was mostly covered instead of destroyed.

Hagia Sofia is surrounded by two major mosques, both well worth seeing. The other must-see is Topkapi, better known as the Seraglio, the sultan's administrative and residential palace, famous for its harem. Besides the architecture and artwork, I remember there was a room with a beautiful fountain. In the Ottoman period, with the fountain always flowing, officials could speak to each other without being overheard. The running water muffled their voices. I can attest, yes, it worked; an ingenious low-tech solution to thwarting spies.

The Grand Bizarre was another must see. It's the original version of a modern mall. There are over 60 streets of covered market stalls. It's overwhelming. Since I am not a shopper, I didn't stay long. Nonetheless, after strolling through the Grand Bizarre, other similar markets anywhere in the world can't quite compete.

On subsequent trips, I was taken to see interesting places by local bankers. The Bosporus Bridge was the first bridge built to cross the straight. It had been completed about 10 years before my first visit. On one trip, I was taken to a restaurant on the Asian side. To get there, we drove across the bridge. Today, it's no big deal because there are several similar bridges. However, then it still felt novel. A series of small restaurants lined the waterfront. The restaurant my hosts chose wasn't fancy, but it was definitely authentic, serving local fish dishes.

One Sunday, when I was in Istanbul, I went to Mass. Finding a Roman Catholic church was a bit of a challenge. The closest was inside an embassy compound, behind high walls.

As I would find in Muslim country after Muslim country, although purportedly religiously tolerant, tolerance only went so far. Orthodox churches were not very visible in Istanbul, even though Istanbul, formerly Constantinople, had been the heart of Orthodox Christianity until the 20th century, when Turkey and Greece signed the Treaty of Lausanne, ending their war, which began right after WW I. The treaty defined the borders of Greece and Turkey, requiring the movement of vast numbers of Christians from Turkey to Greece and Muslims from Greece to Turkey. A similar program of mass ethnic *expulsions* would be repeated decades later in the Indian subcontinent, only on a grander scale.

Following my trips to Turkey, I usually went to Israel because of direct flights to Tel Aviv. I learned from Israelis that there was a vibrant Jewish community in Turkey, which may help explain the traditional warm relations between the two countries, at least until recently. On my first trip to Israel, what shocked me the most, was the amount of security needed to board a plane to Tel Aviv.

Elsewhere, airport security was still light. Today, airport security checks might not be quite as severe as when going to Israel, but they are getting pretty close.

Israel

Arriving at Ben Gurion Airport was much easier. When going through customs and immigration, I asked that my passport not be stamped, because an Israeli stamp in my passport would have precluded me from visiting most Arab countries. The officials were used to such requests. It was no big deal.

When I arrived at my hotel in Tel Aviv, along the oceanfront, I could have been at any US beach resort. Everything was modern and clean. This would be the first of many trips there. My views of the Palestinian-Israeli conflict would change radically as time passed.

The US Embassy was just a short distance from the hotel. It seemed small to me. The meetings there went as usual. I met with Israeli bankers. Meeting government officials would have to wait until Jerusalem. On Friday, I took a taxi from Tel Aviv to Jerusalem. It wasn't a long ride. My driver was loquacious, so I got a short history about the significance of the road we were on, along with explanations about how the 1967 War made this route possible. Some of the land along the route had previously been Palestinian-Jordanian territory, or beyond the *Green Line*, the formal demarcation line drawn up by the UN, between Israel and Transjordan. We tend to forget that before 1967 War, the West Bank was part of Transjordan.

Driving this road from the coast to Jerusalem made it easy to understand the biblical phrase, "going up to

Jerusalem." It involved a steady uphill climb, along a winding road. On this trip, I stayed at the King David Hotel, an iconic Jerusalem landmark, at the heart of a now reunited city. Prior to 1967, it was close to the border dividing East and West Jerusalem. It's a large stone building. I was immediately told about the hotel's historical significance in the Israeli fight to oust the British. In July 1946, the Irgun, an extreme right-wing group within the Jewish resistance forces, blew up an entire corner of the hotel. The hotel was being used as the British Mandate administrative center. About 90 people were killed either inside or near the hotel when the bomb exploded. In the 1980s, the hotel showed no signs of the damage done decades before.

Since I arrived on a Friday afternoon, preparations were underway for Shabbat, or the Jewish Sabbath. From Friday night until Saturday evening, there would be no restaurant service in this Jerusalem hotel, except with food prepared before the Sabbath began. I was quite familiar with Jewish dietary laws from my time in Canada when I shared an apartment with a Kosher-observant student. However, it was here that I saw my first *Sabbath elevator*. Orthodox Jews are precluded from all work on the Sabbath, and taken to the extreme, many won't even press elevator buttons after sundown. During Shabbat, the elevators stopped automatically on every floor, with the door opening and closing on its own. The same was true for light switches. Timers had made things easier for everyone involved.

Since Shabbat is usually celebrated at home, there were practically no guests eating in the hotel, except for non-Jewish foreigners. It was eerily quiet. That's when I had a chance to chat with the staff, which was almost exclusively Palestinian. It was after hearing their individual stories that I became quite sympathetic to their cause. That view would change as the years passed.

Jerusalem was not dangerous in those early years. You could walk wherever you liked, with little fear. That first evening, I decided to walk through the Old City. The streets were absolutely deserted. You could hear people talking in their apartments, but no one was on the street. It was truly spooky. I later learned that although this was typical of Jerusalem on the Sabbath, it was very different in Tel Aviv, which handled the Sabbath, let's say, *in a less rigid manner*.

The next morning, I decided to do some sightseeing. I walked throughout the Old City once again, exploring the many historic religious sites. That's when I learned that the *Wailing Wall* was no longer called that, but now was referred to as the *Western Wall*, or the western wall of the Jewish Temple destroyed by the Romans in 70 AD. That also marked the date when the Romans ousted the Jews from Judea.

Later, when in Italy, I learned from scholars that with new information gathered from studying the structure of the Colosseum itself, it was not just built with the treasure taken from the Temple, which was well known, but it was also built by Jewish slaves brought to Rome following the Siege of Jerusalem. We can see various references to Jerusalem and Jews on the Arch of Titus, near the Forum in Roman, which was built to celebrate the conquest.

Until recently, the Menorah was the traditional symbol representing Jews and Judea, not the Star-of-David. The specific design of the Star-of-David is a new symbol designed a few hundred years ago, not that any of this makes a difference.

The Western Wall is at the base of one of Islam's holiest sites, the Dome of the Rock. Muslims believe that Mohammed ascended into heaven after touching his foot to a stone at the center of the mosque. There is an indentation there, which I could clearly see. Jews believe that this is where the last Temple stood. In some ways, it is one of the most dangerous places on earth because some ultra-orthodox Jews want to rebuild the temple on this site. That would entail destroying the Dome of the Rock. Catastrophe would ensue. However, according to many scholars, the Temple was not located there, but slightly to the South. Muslim claims to Temple Mount refer not to specifically naming it in the Koran, but because Mohammed is believed to have *visited the furthest mosque*, which they interpret as meaning a mosque in Jerusalem. Jewish and Christian scholars point out that when Mohammed died, there was a Christian church on the site. A mosque was only built there years later. My conclusion is that none of these issues will be resolved anytime soon. I am glad I am not a religious scholar or an archeologist. In the Holy Land, those can be dangerous occupations.

In the post-1973 period, Israel, as was true in many other countries around the world, suffered from low growth. By the early 1980s, the Israeli economy was reeling from ever-accelerating inflation because fiscal policy was expansive, and price indexation was embedded throughout the economy. By 1984, inflation was recorded in the triple-digit level. As noted in my description of Argentina, hyperinflation demonetizes an economy, causing a sharp drop in the real money supply. Unless drastic measures are taken, the economy quickly heads towards collapse, in mid-1985, the Israeli government adopted a major structural reform program. It included price controls, wage increase limitations negotiated with the trade unions, cut the budget deficit sharply and limited the Bank of Israel's ability to print money to fund the government deficit. The shekel/pound was devalued. Besides the domestic program, the stabilization program was enhanced by massive US economic aid of $3 billion per year in grants, not loans. To put this into perspective, if the US provided a similar level of aid to Mexico during the 1982 crisis, on a per capita basis, aid to Mexico would have totaled about $27 billion (close to the amount eventually given to help Mexico a decade later). The combination of a well-designed domestic stabilization program and $3 billion in grants from the US proved very successful. The economy increasingly followed capitalist norms. The country reaped the benefits from these changes starting in the 1990s.

For years, Israel had been moving to the right politically. A major reason for the drift towards the right was the post-1967 War outcome Israel faced. It was suddenly occupying land where a large number of Palestinians lived. Such occupation created tensions on both sides. Many found it better to have stricter rules regarding Palestinians living in these newly occupied lands. In addition, the rightward drift was increased by the demographic drift that had been underway for many years. A growing proportion of Israelis were *Sephardi* or *Oriental Jews*, to a point where they represented a majority of Israeli Jews. Most Sephardim either came from Middle Eastern countries or were the descendants of Middle Eastern immigrants. These Oriental Jews were comfortable with a more authoritarian government than the Ashkenazim or those who came from Europe. When I started visiting Israel, the Likud, a rightwing party under Menachem Begin, had been in power since 1973.

That's when I first learned about Judea and Samaria, the names used by the Likud for the West Bank territories. I was often told by Israelis, off the record, that these territories would eventually be transformed into Jewish territory. This seemed a pipedream. In retrospect, those people were prescient. Jerusalem was considered a different issue. For Israelis, then and now, the top priority was to build settlements encircling Jerusalem, guaranteeing it as Israel's capital.

Before the First Intifada, traveling around the West Bank was easy. On my first weekend in Jerusalem, I took a taxi to Bethlehem, which was just a short ride away. I was surprised at its proximity to Jerusalem, a mere six-miles. There were no checkpoints along the way.

The little town appeared prosperous, with souvenir shops bordering Manger Square. Historically, it was a Christian city, but as elsewhere in the West Bank, Muslims were becoming the majority.

The de-Christianization of the Holy Land has been caused by multiple factors. One is that Christians had close connections with the West through their church affiliations. Many school teachers were from Western religious orders. This gave Palestinian Christians access to help when they decided to emigrate. They emigrated because there was little economic opportunity in the West Bank. In addition, historical religious strife between Muslims and Christians continued unabated. Those Christians who could emigrate, emigrated in large numbers. There is a growing concern that there will be few Christian left, not just there, but throughout the Middle East.

In Manger Square, there were Israeli soldiers standing guard along the rooves. The church above the traditional site of Jesus' birth was nothing spectacular, especially compared with churches in Western Europe. Going downstairs, you came upon a grotto with a small altar, below which was a star, marking the spot where the faithful believe Jesus was born. Mass tourism hadn't yet arrived. There were no long lines, and no limits on how long you could stay and pray.

Major Christian religious sites in the Holy Land were occupied by the Orthodox, with Roman Catholic and other non-Protestant Christian denominations sharing the space. In the case of the Church of the Nativity, this meant that the Greek Orthodox, Armenian Orthodox and Roman Catholics each had their own monasteries on the site.

Near Bethlehem was Rachel's Tomb, a tomb revered by Jews, Christians and Muslims. I have been told that today you can no longer approach the tomb from the West Bank side, because of the security wall.

After passing Rachel's tomb, I had my tax driver take me to Hebron. Even in those years, Hebron was not a safe place. The Tomb of the Patriarchs, revered by Jews, Christians and Muslims is the traditional burial site for Abraham and Sarah, Isaac and Rebecca and Jacob and Leah, three of the most important Old Testament biblical couples.

Except for Temple Mount, it was the only multi-religious site I identified as controlled by Muslims, the reason being that the tombs are underneath a mosque. Non-Muslims were not allowed to visit the shrine until the 20th century.

Hebron was and is the largest West Bank city. It always had a small Jewish population, but in 1929, Arab riots resulted in the deaths of about 65 Jewish men, women and children. They destroyed Jewish homes. It wasn't until 1968 that a few Jews returned. The relationship between the Muslim and Jewish communities in Hebron remained strained. Eventually an agreement was reached which divided Hebron into Muslim and Jewish quarters. Nevertheless, tensions were high even on my first trip there.

The next day, I visited the Church of the Holy Sepulcher, the church where tradition has it as the place where Jesus was crucified and buried. It is one of the strangest church structures I have seen anywhere in the world. It is a hodge-podge of non-Protestant Christian denominations. It's religious chaos under one roof.

As usual, pride of place went to the Orthodox Church. The Roman Catholic Church has a separate chapel off to the side of the holiest site. Behind the sacred spot, the Copts have their own section. I'm not sure exactly where the Armenians were located, but I often saw them processing up and down a major stairway in the church. To make matters even more confusing, the church keys are held by a Muslim. I did not find Jerusalem to be a place where I would care to stay for a religious experience. Religious tourism, yes, spiritual fulfillment, no.

Everywhere I went in Jerusalem, I was disappointed by what I saw. The Via Dolorosa, or the traditional route taken by Jesus prior to His crucifixion, might bring devotion to many, but not to me. It was far too *touristy*. I had already visited many other Christian pilgrimage sites, where I felt far more *spiritual*.

I remember going to the Mount of Olives, the traditional site where Jesus prayed before Good Friday. My reaction upon seeing that iconic view of Jerusalem from across the valley below was to ask myself, "Why have people fought over this land for millennia?" It just didn't seem worth it. It was beyond me. I guess I realized that I don't believe particular places on earth are any more spiritual than others. It's what's inside the human heart that counts.

I would visit Israel on several occasions for work, but I also went once just to see all the other Christian sites outside Jerusalem. I had the same reaction. It was nice to see all these places, but for me the fascination with the Holy Land was purely intellectual and historical. Please don't mistake my lack of feeling for the Holy Land as a rejection of Christian spirituality. It isn't. I had already developed a spirituality that transcends time and place.

Most of my trips to Israel happened when I worked for Irving Trust, but when I was at Moody's, I was asked to be the lead analyst for the first bond rating for the Israeli Government. What was special about that trip was that I was traveling with two of my favorite Moody's colleagues, David Levey and Ken Pinkes. David was (is I suppose still) a Jewish atheist. Ken was, what I would call, a lapsed Roman Catholic. I enjoyed being able to show them around Jerusalem, a city I now knew pretty well. I believe that after that trip, David did not suddenly become a believer, but I do think that he regained respect for his family's religious traditions. Our discussions during our walks along the Tel Aviv beach were profound.

I have kept a fondness for Israel. As I mentioned earlier, my views regarding Israel changed as the years passed. The main reason was that although sympathetic to Palestinian issues, the first and then second intifadas showed me that there would never be peace between these two peoples. I slowly realized it wasn't the fault of Israelis alone. Most of the blame relates to Arab and Muslim history. If an accord is ever signed between Israel and the Palestinian Authority, it would only be a sham peace accord. This change in mindset developed as I traveled repeatedly to Muslim countries in the region and learned much more about Islam.

Egypt

Irving Trust had major correspondent banking relationships with all the big Egyptian banks. That made trips to Egypt a necessity. Cairo was, and is, a crowded city, packed with more history than almost anywhere else on earth. It is populated by some of the kindest people I ever met during my travels. It was always a pleasure to visit Egypt.

What first struck me when I arrived at one of the few luxury hotels in Cairo, was how friendly the staff was. I soon learned that this was simply the Egyptian way. The kindness and gentleness I experienced from everyone was incredible. This was a far cry from the poor service I usually received from Israelis in Tel Aviv restaurants. I was told poor service in Israel, excluding the Palestinian staff, resulted from the lack of a Jewish service tradition. Anyway, that sounded good to me.

The shortage of hotels was a major challenge in traveling to Cairo in the early 1980s. There were only three big hotels for foreigners; the Hilton, the Sheraton and Shepheards, a hotel dating from the 1840s. The original hotel burned down in a fire caused by riots during the 1952 Revolution. A new hotel was built, near the original site, but was nowhere as nice as the two big chain hotels.

Two Irving Trust colleagues told me that on one trip, when arriving in Cairo, the reservation for one of them had been lost. They were forced to share a hotel room, which they still complained about years later. As with Istanbul, many more hotels would appear in just a few short years.

On a clear day, you could see the pyramids from downtown Cairo. Traffic was bad, but not as bad as Mexico City. On my first trip to Cairo, I arrived on a weekend and planned to take a tour of Cairo and its surroundings. By this time, as my income had been increasing, I was able to hire personal guides instead of taking bus tours. The difference between the two types of tours is significant. I was able to see much more because there was no time wasted getting all the other tourists back on the bus, an often-slow process. Personal tours became my modes operandi from then on, continuing to this day.

On my first trip, I headed off to the pyramids in Giza. What can I say? They are monumental in every sense of that word, one being as high as about fifty stories. Then I heard the story that the Sphinx had survived pretty much intact for millennia, but lost its nose in the 18th century, as a result of French soldiers using it for target practice. As is often the case, this common explanation was not true. Instead, the nose was destroyed in the 14th century by an iconoclastic Muslim leader. Also, I was told that scholars believed the Sphinx to be much older than the pyramids.

Once outside of central Cairo, you could easily see where irrigation ended and where the desert began. The transition was stark, going from green to brown. After the

Giza plateau, my guide took me to Saqqara, where the world's oldest still standing pyramid is located. The five-thousand-year-old Step Pyramid marked a major innovation in architecture. Beyond the pyramid itself, there was a colonnade, which are the world's first columns, another Egyptian innovation. It was then that I realized that, although I had believed that Greece and Rome were ancient, and they are, compared to Egypt, they are just parvenus.

Another place the guide took me, which would not have been possible for a tour group, was to an underground tomb, where sacred bulls were buried. They were truly huge sarcophagi. I learned that these massive sarcophagi were made from stone found about 500 miles from this location. The ancient Egyptians somehow were able to transport them to here and get them underground. The significance of the engineering required was demonstrated by one of the sarcophagi, which was at an angle in the middle of the corridor. My guide explained that when the first king of modern Egypt died in the 19th century, people wanted to bury him in one of these sarcophagi. However, they couldn't move it more than a few feet. Quite telling!

Following visits to the monuments, my guide insisted on me riding a camel. I was young, so I said, yes. I never realized getting on a camel could be so harrowing. First, the animal bent its front legs allowing me to climb onto the saddle. Then, the camel got up. Getting up produced a catapult-like action. I felt that I was going to be thrown right off the camel. I held on for dear life. Then the camel driver decided that I would enjoy having the camel race around a bit. Suddenly I felt like I was flying. Needless to say, the camel driver thought all this amusing. I still have the pictures of me riding my one and only camel.

I didn't visit the Egyptian Museum until the following trip. Then I stayed at the Hilton, which was next door to the museum. On a weekend, I visited the museum, which was spectacular. There was hallway after hallway filled with ancient Egyptian art. What was most stunning was visiting the room where the King Tut exhibit was. When this had traveled around the world people would wait for hours to see it. Yet, here I was in a small room with just a few people. There was no wait. I doubt I could do that so easily today.

Several trips later, I was able to tour the famous Christian sites, with the Hanging Church of the Virgin Mary being the most famous. When I visited it, it was suffering from severe water damage resulting from rising ground water. It almost looked like the Nile had moved into the church. Since my visit, I have heard that the church has been completely renovated.

Egypt's Islamic history is complicated, to say the least. The Arabs were able to conquer Egypt in large part because Egyptian Copts had rejected the Council of Chalcedon's pronouncement on the nature of Jesus. They were then viewed as heretics by Orthodox Christians based in Constantinople. This on-going religious dispute caused a rift between the Coptic Church and the Greek Orthodox Church. When the Arabs arrived, the Coptic Pope preferred signing a peace treaty with the Arabs relegating the Copts to second-class status rather than accept direction from Constantinople. The irony is that in 1973, both Coptic and the Greek Orthodox Churches realized it was just a semantic issue. Now most recognize that the Copts are not really monophysites but have a view of Christ that is similar to the Orthodox view. It was just thirteen centuries too late.

It took centuries before the majority of Egyptians became Muslim. Even as recently as fifty years ago, it was estimated that about 20-25 percent of Egypt's population was Coptic. Many Egyptian Muslims told me that Copts were viewed by most Egyptians as the *real Egyptians*, because they have preserved the country's pre-invasion language and pre-invasion religion. In recent decades, as Islamic extremism has grown, so has persecution of Copts. Most Copts eligible to emigrate to the West are doing just that, causing a sharp decline in the percentage of the Egyptian population that is still Christian. The same is true in country after country across the Middle East. A similar exodus of Jews occurred during the first decades following Israeli independence. It got too dangerous for most to remain in Muslim countries.

Egypt is incredibly crowded. Population growth is the main constraint on its politics and economics. For millennia, the fertile Nile Basin was the breadbasket of the Mediterranean Basin. The country was able to export massive amounts of food because it had a small population relative to its agricultural output. During Roman times, Egypt's population was about 3 million. By 1800, it is estimated to have had slightly less than 4 million people. By 1900, that more than doubled to about 10 million. The very latest estimates put the population at slightly below 100 million, a ten-fold increase in about 120 years. Water availability constrains the amount of arable land. From being one of the wealthiest countries for millennia, it is now among the poorer. It is a social and political disaster waiting to happen.

During my visits both for Irving Trust and Moody's, the main sources of foreign exchange were oil and gas-related exports, tourism, emigrant remittances, Suez Canal revenues and foreign aid. The biggest change to take place since then is the surge in emigrant remittances. The latest numbers put remittances at about $20 billion, dwarfing all other sources of foreign exchange.

Visiting Egyptian offices usually provided little information. The data was dated and often opaque. The reality was that for Irving Trust, at least, the key issue related to short-term risk, which was not insignificant. The bank maintained most correspondent banks relationships during my tenure, but under strict limits. At Moody's, the first rating was issued in 1996. It was two notches below investment grade. The rating declined seriously at Moody's following the events of the so-called Arab Spring, one of the greatest disasters for the Arab world in recent decades.

There had been quite a bit of optimism in financial markets regarding Egypt's future after the country signed its historic peace treaty with Israel in 1979. However, that optimism was reduced when President Sadat was assassinated in 1981.

Most of Egypt's elites didn't particularly care for his replacement, Hosni Mubarak. I was told by people that he looked like a monkey. In a society where form and grace mattered, he was viewed as too crude. I was told on many trips that he would only be a temporary president until the military found someone better. Well their predictions about Mubarak's longevity were totally wrong since he lasted until 2011 and the beginning of the Arab Spring.

I met with foreign academics living in Cairo. The best meetings took place on a Nile houseboat, where one of the academics lived. Given the crowded conditions of Cairo, there were a few people lucky enough to live on the river itself. It looked pretty cushy to me. It was there that I first heard that Egyptians looked down on the rest of the Arab world. They saw themselves, first as Egyptians, and then as Arabs. I was told Egyptians despised the rich Gulf Arabs, who except for recent oil income, were nothing more than glorified Bedouins. That helped me understand the degree of tension that existed then, and still exists, between Egypt and the Gulf states. Simply put, Egypt considers itself the intellectual and cultural center of the Arab world. This pride in their background made survival in the modern world, often under often terrible conditions, endurable.

The biggest single social problem was and is caused by the housing shortage. The Egyptian tradition is that a couple would only marry if they can afford their own apartment. Unless that has changed in recent years, it means that marriages are often postponed for years, or might never happen at all. This problem is exacerbated by a society with strict rules against premarital sex. I leave it to your imagination to envision the consequences. This problem is mirrored in a number of Arab countries, with Algeria probably being the next worst in this regard.

When I first visited Egypt, the majority of women on the streets wore western-style clothing. None of those women wore the traditional headscarf. As time passed, I began to see more and more women wear more traditional clothing, especially the headscarf. I learned from some female officials I met with, that wearing the scarf reduced the likelihood they would be harassed by men either on the street or at work. Even if they weren't particularly pious, wearing a headscarf made life easier for them. A similar development would occur across the Middle East. It became easier for women to simply wear a headscarf.

Wearing a headscarf has become associated only with Islam. However, when I was young, outside the home, women always wore a scarf or a hat on their head. You may even have seen photos of Queen Elizabeth wearing a scarf when walking outdoors in the countryside.

Modesty in dress was the norm in the West until the 1960s. Before then, headscarves (not burqas) worn by Muslim women would have gone unnoticed. Roman Catholic nuns wore clothing that is similar to a burqa, except a nun's face was never covered. No hair was supposed to be visible. Roman Catholic women had to cover their head when going to church. It's the West that moved away from any modicum of modesty, rather than Islam suddenly inventing more modest dress. It's always odd how quickly we forget our own history.

Yugoslavia

Another country I started visiting while at Irving Trust was Yugoslavia, a country that no longer exists. Correspondent banking was key. I made regular trips there from 1979 to the late 1980s. Usually I went to Belgrade, the country's capital.

Around 1980, Yugoslavia was well-known for its more moderate version of Communism. The reason for Yugoslav independence had more to do with how the Germans were defeated, than because it was a bright star for innovation. Unlike other Eastern European states, which were liberated from the Nazis by the Soviet Red Army, Yugoslavs had such a strong partisan army that they did not need the Soviet Union to expel the Nazis. The partisans were made up of Communists and its supporters. This was in stark contrast to some Croatians who adopted Nazi policies.

After the war, the country fell under the control of Tito. His father was a Croat, his mother Slovenian. He fought in World War I as a soldier in the Hapsburg military. He was caught by the Russians and was sent prison in Russia. He soon began to take part in the Communist Revolution there. Later when he returned home, it was to the newly created country of Yugoslavia, an odd amalgamation of various ethnic and religious groups.

He remained active in Yugoslav Communist politics. During WW II, the political situation in Yugoslavia was extremely complicated. There was an extreme right-wing group of Croatians who supported the Nazis, and who established an independent Croatian Nazi puppet state. Tito headed the partisans. Most observers recognized the partisans were the most effective partisan guerrilla group anywhere in Europe during WW II. This strong nationally based guerrilla group did not need the Russians to liberate them. Unlike any other countries in Eastern Europe, the Yugoslavs liberated themselves. Given the internal violence during the war between a pro-Nazi Croatian government and the rest of the country, the government's anathema for nationalist groups was understandable.

Tito established a Communist regime, but in defiance of Stalin, Tito was able to pull Yugoslavia out of Cominform. That enabled him to create a market version of communism, where firms were owned by the workers, but where firms competed using market forces. In the late 1970s and 1980s, visiting Yugoslavia was unlike visiting any other Communist country in Eastern Europe.

Tito had been the unifying force from the end of WW II until his death in 1980. Post-Tito, the Yugoslavs came up with an interesting political solution to the ethnic tension problem. The Presidency would rotate among the Presidents of the various republics.

On my first visit to Belgrade, I stayed at the downtown Moskva Hotel. There was a luxury hotel, the Intercontinental. It wasn't located downtown, so I always preferred the far from luxurious Moskva. It was my first experience with Eastern European socialist architecture. Everything was made to look luxurious, but almost everything was uncomfortable and completely illogical. Since I was a so-called important guest, I got a suite with two floors. At first, I was impressed, but then I realized that the suite was organized in a weird way. Some things were placed on the second floor, which would normally have been found in the main room of a suite. The minifridge was just one example. The bathroom was huge but lacked the normal comforts of a hotel bathroom. The chairs were red velvet with gold leaf, and quite grand, except they were uncomfortable to sit on.

One advantage of staying at the Moskva, besides its location, was that it was uncomfortable, so I rarely stayed inside, forcing me to walk more than I might have otherwise done. Downtown architecture was Stalinesque, complete with drab concrete structures lacking any charm.

My meetings in Belgrade always began with meetings with Beogradska Banka, the country's biggest bank. This relationship proved important in the future in a totally unexpected way.

The Chairman of Beogradska Banka was Slobodan Milosevic. Irving Trust had a suite at the Waldorf Astoria, where important customers were entertained. On several occasions, Milosevic was there as guest of honor. I usually attended these dinner parties. In retrospect, Milosevic is the only convicted war criminal I have ever met. Unfortunately, I can't say I saw anything wrong with his behavior at those dinners. He was pleasant and entertaining.

Beogradska Banka was always a good source for economic and political information. It had a professional economics department. Meeting with government officials was less valuable.

On one of my early trips, it was suggested that I should visit several of the republics to better understand the country. After a stop in Belgrade, I went to Zagreb in Croatia.

I already knew lots about Croatia because my local Roman Catholic Church in New York was staffed by Croatian Franciscans. The original American parish had been called St. Raphael. The church building was and still is magnificent. It was known in times past as the *Cathedral of the West Side*. A large interior with massive and beautiful stained-glass windows needed to be preserved. Robert Moses had destroyed large swathes of the far West Side of New York, so St. Rafael had few parishioners left in the depopulated neighborhood. The New York Archdiocese came up with the ingenious idea of combining the Croatian Saints Cyril and Methodius parish with St. Raphael. That area today is filled to capacity with huge high-rise apartment towers, a far cry from the early 1980s, when it looked almost bombed-out. The priests didn't speak English well. They asked me to write biblical commentaries, in English, on the Sunday readings, which were published in the weekly bulletin. I did that for years, hence my familiarity with Croatia. I was by then far from my early anticlericalism.

After Croatia, I went to Ljubljana, the capital of Slovenia. Slovenia was a surprise because it looked like a slightly poorer version of Austria, and not like either Croatia or Serbia. This small republic was vital to Yugoslavia's economic success, accounting for about 40 percent of total Yugoslav exports. It was much more sophisticated than the other republics.

From Slovenia, I took a train ride, via Belgrade, to Sarajevo, the capital of Bosnia-Herzegovina. This was the most interesting part of my visit. Sarajevo was a picturesque city. I would be staying at the hotel where Archduke Franz Ferdinand stayed just before his assassination in 1914. As you know, that triggered the start of World War I. I don't think the hotel had been updated much since then.

The strangest thing I saw in Sarajevo was a museum dedicated to Gavrilo Princip, the 19-year-old assassin of the Archduke and his wife. I never saw a museum anywhere in the world dedicated to an assassin. Outside the museum, a short distance away were two foot prints etched into the sidewalk, indicating the exact spot from which Princip fired his shots. The explanation given for the museum was that the assassination eventually resulted in the creation of Yugoslavia after the war. Bizarre. The museum no longer exists. It was a victim of the Bosnian civil war.

Although the museum was a curiosity, the really fascinating part of my stay there was a luncheon hosted by local bankers. It was organized to make sure I understood how the various Bosnian groups got along. Each participant told me about their family background. Almost all were either the offspring of mixed marriages among Serbs, Croats, Slovenians and Bosnians, or were married to members of different Yugoslav ethnic groups. Only one of the bankers was Muslim. Since I already knew a lot about how Croatians interpreted Yugoslav history, I was not taken in by such displays of domestic ethnic tranquility. What I have found most disturbing about that luncheon is that I assume many, if not most of the attendees probably later died during the civil war or were forced to become refugees. Those memories are a vivid reminder that ethnic wars are easily triggered, with unpredictable outcomes.

By the mid-1980s, the Yugoslav economy was under severe stress. Since short-term risk was key to Irving Trust's business there, getting a handle on the country's international reserves was vital. That didn't prove easy. I had access to the published statistics; however, I had heard from colleagues that some of the reserves were not really genuine international reserves. It was thought the government had begun to include debts owed by African countries as international reserve assets.

It was no surprise that a government might try to manipulate its international reserves. Prior to the East Asian crisis in 1997, the best example was Peru. Peru would borrow money from Deutsche Bank, and then repay it the following day. It was deposited in the bank just long enough to report the deposit as reserves at month-end. Such deception doesn't work for long, and usually results in a bigger problem once the deception is discovered. Irving Trust took an increasingly conservative approach to Yugoslavia.

Stock Market Crash

In October 1987, the stock market crashed, with the Dow falling by 22.6 percent in one day. There was panic spiraling throughout financial markets. There are many theories about what caused the depth of the fall. I can provide one that was provided to me by Peter Palmieri, Vice Chairman and Chief Credit Officer of ITC. We had become close professional partners. I had regular access to his office.

The afternoon of the crash, I stopped by his office on the 10th floor. He was sitting at his desk. When he looked up and saw me, he waved for me to come into his office. He then told me something quite incredible. He said he just got a call from the Fed. From his next statement, I assumed the call came from the President of the New York Fed. He said, "I just got a call from the Fed telling us to lend! That's exactly what we will do." Other large banks were obviously getting similar calls.

Peter explained that markets were crashing so much because there was fear that Solomon Bros. might go under because of massive losses it had experienced that day. The financial system was about to freeze up, much like what happened decades later with the sudden collapse of Lehman Bros in 2008. However, in a time when financial markets were opaquer, and when the Fed could influence events far more than today, that series of phone calls to bankers stopped the crisis dead in its tracks. Everything quickly went back to normal. If the Lehman

Bros crisis could have been dealt with like the Solomon Bros crisis, perhaps the Great Recession could have been avoided.

I am against complete transparency for the banking system. It is not a positive. During the 1980s, as I learned by sitting on bank credit committees, banks usually maintained *hidden reserves*. In other words, they didn't always present mark-to-market measures of assets. Banks in trouble would be known to the Fed and other regulators and could be dealt with. However, this was not the real benefit of hidden reserves. The real benefit was that large banks were able to smooth their earnings from quarter to quarter. The Swiss banks were leaders in this regard. Large American banks did the same thing, but slightly less aggressively than the Swiss.

The usual way to keep reserves hidden was to ignore price appreciation of bank real estate, often its headquarters, although any asset might be used for this purpose. When the bank was doing exceptionally well, more assets were hidden. However, most importantly, when quarterly profits for operating revenue was off the mark, a revaluation of other assets would keep the income stream relatively stable. Regulated bank stocks were almost similar to regulated utility stocks, both of which were considered low risk investments. This was at the heart of banking from the end of WW II until the late 1980s. Banking crises were minor during that period. After 1989, financial crises have kept coming with greater frequency and severity. Total transparency at large US banks and at the Federal Reserve is not a healthy development. Some things are better addressed behind closed doors.

An earlier example of the importance of opacity in banking was the November 1985 Bank of New York computer glitch that would have seized financial markets except for an extraordinary discount window loan peaking at just below $30 billion or about 150 percent of its assets. Technically, the Fed shouldn't have done this, but the safety of the whole system was at risk. The computer problem wasn't fully resolved for a number of days. Of course, Fed officials were still dragged before Congress to testify about the matter. Once again, this is an example where total transparency would not have been good. This was handled, and the public was not hurt by this special intervention. I doubt this could happen so quickly in today's *bare-all* world.

Bank of New York

In late 1988, Irving Trust was taken over by the Bank of New York (BoNY) in the only hostile takeover of a major bank in US history. Given its problems in 1985, it's not surprising that the Bank of New York wanted to get access to Irving Trust's state-of-the-art data processing center on Barclay Street. Besides the overall security of the system, this would enable the bank to enter correspondent banking in a big way. For one year, Irving Trust tried to end the takeover bid. It didn't succeed. Irving Trust employees were devastated. The two banks had very different cultures. Irving Trust employees viewed themselves as highly qualified bankers, with a culture somewhat similar to J.P. Morgan. Bank of New York was viewed as a pedestrian institution, far below Irving Trust's league. It felt like a barbarian takeover. In many respects, that proved to be the case.

Soon after completing the merger, all Irving Trust employees were interviewed by Bank of New York officers. The result for the economics department was devastating. BoNY fired the entire staff except for me and two assistants. We went from an amazing economics team to a one-man show. I made the cut, but I was far from ecstatic about the result.

My first introduction to BoNY senior management involved how to handle a senior member of the former economics team. He was still on medical leave following complications from brain surgery. I was told by the then President of the bank, that my former colleague would be fired while still on medical leave. I argued strongly against that. I told him that would send out a terrible signal to other employees. In the end, Renyi relented, and said that the economist would be let go when he came off medical leave. I felt good that at least I had bought my former colleague some time to help him and his family adjust to much changed circumstances. Nonetheless, just the idea of firing someone while on medical leave was a far cry from Irving Trust's culture.

Civil War

In the late 1980s, developments in Yugoslavia were reaching a fever pitch. Kosovo was becoming a bigger and bigger problem. Slovenia and Croatia were increasingly unhappy that Milosevic, now the President of Serbia, intended to create a Greater Serbia.

In early 1990, I received a phone call from the senior economist at Beogradska Banka. He asked if he could stop by my office. He had never visited me in New York before. When he arrived, he appeared somewhat distraught.

He told me, "It's all over."

I asked what he meant. He said the week before; the Slovenians had walked out of a Communist Party conference. He went on to say this meant there would soon be an all-out civil war between Croatia and Serbia. He confessed that only Slovenia had been able to keep tensions between the two republics below the boiling point. He added, "Now that the Slovenians have left, no one can stop a coming civil war." He then explained the reason for his in-person visit. He wanted me to know that if I returned to Belgrade, he would no longer be able to tell me the truth. He wanted me to know that in advance. Another Wow moment. BoNY stopped doing business there.

Hungary

Another Eastern European I visited regularly was Hungary. In the 1980s, it was still a Communist country, following communist economic policies. Budapest, even then, was a beautiful city. The hills of Buda are great. The bridges connecting Buda with Pest were quaint. The government buildings on the Pest side looked old but were not. The original building had been destroyed. These buildings were exact copies of the originals. The center of the city looked like it was out of a fairy tale.

The hotel was modern and equal to any in the West. Everything was inexpensive. The food was delicious, as was the wine.

The officials I met with were highly qualified. Their main complaint was that Hungary's debt was only large because the country refused to default when other countries, not only in Latin America, but in Eastern Europe, defaulted. He made a good argument about the country's willingness to meet its obligations on time, even if the cost to Hungarians was high.

Most countries around the world were negatively affected by rising oil prices in 1973, which then was followed by another spike in prices after the 1979 Iranian Revolution. As a resource poor country, Hungary felt the full force of rising energy prices. As Hungary was looking towards Yugoslavia, with which it shared a border. Hungarians had already tried to emulate the Yugoslav approach to

Communism by slowly adding market forces to the centrally planned system. It didn't work. However, the call for reform continued. By the 1980s, inflation was rising rapidly. People on fixed incomes were severely disadvantaged, in particular pensioners. On every visit I would hear about, and actually witness a significant number of elderly people on the streets asking for food. Some went as far as to go through dumpsters.

Hungarians grew increasingly unhappy with so-called Goulash Communism, where a variety of different reforms were implemented, but never in a genuinely thorough program. By the late 1980s, it was obvious that Hungarian Communism was on its last legs. Initially, the government allowed Hungarians to travel abroad more freely. Also, the government dismantled the border fence between Austria and Hungary. Since East Germans were not allowed to visit the West, but were free to travel to Hungary, Hungary suddenly became a major way East Germans were able to leave East Germany. This contributed to rapid the collapse that would take place in East Germany itself.

As usual, Irving Trust kept its correspondent banking, but preferred to stay away from medium-term lending. Hungarians' strong *willingness to pay*, made an economic situation, which was far from ideal, an acceptable risk in the short-term.

One of the best insights I got into the reason for the success of the Austro-Hungarian Empire, was from taking the *Oriental Express*, which at that time, was simply a train that ran from Vienna to Istanbul. I learned that there were many versions of this famous train route. Boarding the train in Vienna, I would get off in Budapest.

The change in scenery was informative. For a while, after departing Vienna, there were mountains and hills. Then suddenly, after crossing the Hungarian border, the landscape changed dramatically. The land was flat and there were farms in all directions. I was now traveling across the famous Hungarian Plain.

It became clear that the union of Austria and Hungary was totally complementary. The Hungarian Plain would produce the food, and money would be made by supplying products to Vienna, a major city. It was a symbiotic relationship made visible by simply looking out train windows.

The Soviet Union

In the 1980s, it was becoming more evident that Communism wasn't an economic success. However, I didn't believe that the Soviet Union would soon collapse. There was one person who predicted that, and he was ITC's CEO, Joe Rice. He was originally an engineer before befriending the then President of Irving Trust, as they shared long commutes from northern Westchester County. That commuting friendship eventually resulted in Irving Trust hiring Mr. Rice. He was extremely intelligent, and always polite and fair, something that would not be matched by BoNY successors.

As CEO, Mr. Rice traveled around the world a lot. Before every foreign trip, the economists handling the countries he would be visiting would give him a briefing on economic and political developments. That way, when he would be in that country, it would appear that he had been following events there very closely. I enjoyed giving him those briefings.

During one of the briefings in the mid-1980s, we were discussing Eastern Europe. It wasn't a lecture by me, but a conversation between the two of us. When we got around to discussing Russia, he surprised me. He said the Soviet Union was going to collapse soon. Why? There were no high-speed cables connecting computers in Leningrad to computers in Moscow. He knew a lot about computer science because not only was he an engineer, but Irving

Trust had just built a state-of-the-art data center, just a short walk from our main office.

He explained part of the reason for the discrepancy was that the US military was far more technologically advanced than the Soviets. He added that the attempt by the Soviets to catch up to US military technology was bankrupting the country. For him, it was only a matter of time before the collapse. This sounded like fantasy. I only took it seriously because I respected his intellect. He turned out to be quite prescient.

My first trip to the USSR was in the late 1980s. Gorbachev was in power. Moscow was a horrible place to visit. Dysfunctional Communism could be seen in all its glory. I stayed in a huge hotel. On every floor, there was a desk where a little old lady sat. She was there to monitor everyone's comings and goings.

Perestroika or restructuring began earnest in 1986. The Soviet economy had been stagnant during the latter Brezhnev years. Something had to be done. The original aim was not to move to a market economy, but rather salvage the reform the Marxist system. That proved a disaster. Economic reforms were moving along as political reforms were underway. Once political reforms became more embedded, then it wasn't long before the Marxist economic system became openly criticized. This turbulence to widespread shortages across the economy. Soviet society was gradually imploding. Crime was already soaring in the city. It was even dangerous at the airports. I was warned to be careful. There were always men outside the hotel trying to exchange money, something that was illegal. I dutifully avoided their offers, even though there was a huge difference between the ruble-dollar exchange rate in the hotel compared to the exchange rate offered on the street.

The real foreign exchange consisted of packs of Marlboro cigarettes. I had been advised to bring several cartons when arriving. That proved to be excellent advice. The first time I went to the hotel restaurant, I was led to my table. After that, nothing happened. No waiter came over, even if called. Then I realized what was needed. I took out a pack of Marlboros, and as if magically, the waiter appeared. My food arrived soon after. Of course, the pack of cigarettes was gone. My meal was billed by the hotel in rubles, but the cigarettes went to the staff. Marlboro cigarettes were as good as gold. Oddly enough, the currency of choice in Romania was a pack of Kent cigarettes. I never learned why there was a difference in the preferred type of cigarettes.

During my free time, I visited some of the close-by historical attractions. I found the G.U.M. department store fascinating. It was famous around the world as Moscow's largest department store. It was a weird place back then. There were small kiosk-like shops where small goods were sold. The place looked half-empty. Another example of a dysfunctional system.

I met with government officials, and more importantly, bankers. The bankers took me to lunch in what was then a new type of restaurant, one that was privately owned. What a difference from the hotel! The food was excellent. I didn't see cigarettes change hands, but I'm sure the bankers knew what needed to be done.

We spent most of our time discussing the changes Gorbachev was making. All the old rules were breaking down. The economy was under major stress. Shortages for the average person were getting worse.

I was told that Gorbachev had been baptized by his grandmother. He was sympathetic to religion, not something that was usual for a Communist leader in Soviet times. He was moving the country to a new model both politically and economically.

The city was drab. It looked really rundown. The people all seemed sullen. It was just a very nice place to visit. I was happy to leave. You could tell how bad off the economy was by the number of passengers on my flights in and out of Moscow. I traveled first class in those days. I was the only first-class passenger going there. I got great service from the crew. On the outbound flight, there were just a few fellow passengers.

In recent years, I have returned to Moscow often. Today, Moscow is utterly different from the 1980s.

The only time I was in Romania was when I took a flight from Budapest to Istanbul. We stopped briefly in Bucharest. The stopover was long enough for us to walk out of the plane. There were a number of Turkish businessmen on the flight. It was nighttime. I asked the Turks where Bucharest was. How come I couldn't see any sign of it? They chuckled. The city was right over there, pointing in a general direction. The reason I couldn't see it was that no lights were on. There was a severe shortage of electricity. The crisis was even worse because not only were there few lights, but heat was also unavailable to most people, despite the cold winter. Romanian Communism was doomed.

Africa

Irving Trust did business in sub-Saharan Africa, but on a small-scale, with the odd exceptions of Ethiopia and Somalia. Since we all knew that for both countries, everything depended on the level of international reserves. Assessing the overall risks were straightforward. Although ITC did business in Ethiopia and Somalia, we took no risks. There was no need for me to visit them. I would have liked to, if only to see the lions which still roamed freely on the palace grounds of Addis Ababa, Ethiopia's capital. It was a tradition started by Haile Selassie.

I wound up learning more about Somalia than I would have ever imagined. One day, my boss arrived at my office along with a young African woman dressed in traditional garb. I was told that since I could speak Italian, I would be working with her while she was at Irving Trust. She only spoke a little English, but she spoke reasonably good Italian. She was the daughter of the Somali President. She would be spending several months with us as an intern.

We got along well. However, I didn't see any evidence of her being interested in economics or banking. I assumed that the President wanted his daughter out of the country. I never heard from her after her short stay with us. I always wondered what happened to her and her family as Somalia plunged into a brutal, and long-lasting civil war.

David Rockefeller and South Africa

By the mid-1980s, events in South Africa showed signs of increased tension. More and more people were calling for boycotts of South Africa. As funds were withdrawn by foreign banks, the country's international liquidity dried up. Eventually, the banks defaulted on their international loans. This prepared the way for the eventual collapse of apartheid.

I didn't travel to South Africa during this time. However, the real end of apartheid South Africa started with David Rockefeller being roundly criticized by friends at Brown University. He was embarrassed by them allowing Chase Manhattan to continue to fund South African institutions. David Rockefeller didn't attend Brown, but he played an active role there because of his father and mother's great love for the university. Both of David's parents were Brown alumni. After that, it became common knowledge within the banking community that Chase would be pulling back from lending there. South African foreign currency liquidity was already tight. The pullout by Chase pushed it over the edge.

I have not traveled extensively in Sub-Saharan Africa. Besides South Africa, I only visited Gabon and Nigeria.

Gabon

Gabon was interesting. The main city and capital, Libreville, sat just beyond the densest tropical rainforest in the world. It was the land of Dr. Schweitzer. It was famous for the number of pygmies who lived in the rain forest. At the same time, with its oil wealth, and close ties to France, visiting Libreville was like visiting an African version of France. The city was modern. The food and hotels were the same as what you could find in France. Some food items were flown in daily from France. The French military had a huge airbase just outside the city. The sound of French military planes taking off and landing was frequent.

The long-time president of the country was named Omar Bongo. He took the name Omar after visiting Ghedaffi and Libya. There he decided to convert to Islam. He was extremely short. As a result, to avoid embarrassment, he banned the use of the term pygmy. I am not making this up.

The most interesting part of the trip was meeting with the national oil company. It was professionally run, with a lot of support from the French. I was told by the staff that exploring for oil was extremely expensive because much of the oil was under lands, which were heavily covered by water and vegetation. The only way to explore for oil, at a time before satellite images, was for men to hang from helicopters and do whatever you need to do to explore for oil. It was quite risky. I was offered the opportunity to join one of these teams and see what it was like. Needless to say, I declined.

Nigeria

I went directly from Gabon to Nigeria. Doing anything in Nigeria was difficult. ITC called upon fellow bankers from JPMorgan to help with the visit. They had an office in Lagos. They made sure I had a hotel room to stay in and helped with arranging all my appointments. I can't remember the name of the hotel except to say that it was modern, but a totally strange place to stay. Lagos is in a tropical zone, which receives plenty of rainfall. However, as in Western Ireland, water supplies to individuals was not guaranteed. Even at the front desk you were told that water might not always be available for showering. They were right. Sometimes the water flowed in the shower, and other times, it came out as just a dribble. I had told that when water availability got really bad, the hotel diverted the swimming pool water to supply the hotel's own needs.

Another sign of Nigerian efficiency or lack thereof in the 1980s was that I could see a ship half-sunk in the ocean water. I was told that the ship had been carrying cement, and after it partially sank, it was simply left there. The beachfront near the hotel was also famous for something else. During a recent coup, former government leaders were brought to the beach and shot. I never learned if they were buried or simply left there until high-tide.

Going to the JPMorgan office was also enlightening. It was on the main commercial street in Lagos. This still meant that there were open sewers on both sides of the street. They looked like ditches that were covered over wherever you needed to cross to get to the building on the other side. I was told by some of the bankers that when it rained heavily, which was frequent, these sewers would overflow.

My meetings with government officials and with the national oil company were not very insightful. One of the most interesting meetings I had was with a Nigerian sociologist. She explained why life in Lagos was so difficult and violent. According to her, the Yoruba people, located where Lagos is, were culturally combative even in the countryside. It was her theory that crowding a naturally combative people into a city like Lagos just acerbated their combativeness. This appeared consistent with my short experience in Lagos. People argued with each other everywhere. Waiters argued in the hotel. Taxi drivers argued with each other. It was really strange to witness.

The city was crime ridden. Precautions had to be taken by my hosts who took me to a restaurant one evening. We had guards accompany us.

I was looking forward to leaving Lagos as soon as possible. I was warned to be careful in the airport. It was not always safe. Anyway, I got through the airport, but only after being *stiffed* for about $50. I was glad to pay that just to leave.

I was going to Cairo. The plane was scheduled to make a stop at Kano in Northern Nigeria. When I boarded in Lagos, there were only about four or five passengers on this big jet, all of us wearing Western clothes. I thought to myself, how can an airline maintain such a flight, with so few passengers? The answer was soon provided. Despite the nearly empty plane, the stewardesses made us sit together at the front of the plane.

Everything changed at Kano. Passengers boarded the plane, taking up every seat. All were dressed in traditional North Nigerian garments, which were flowing and quite colorful. From Cairo, they were going to Mecca for the Hajj. It looked like a flying camel caravan, minus the camels.

All the passengers were polite. The biggest worry was that one of them might try to cook onboard the plane. I was told by a fellow passenger from Lagos that this had happened recently, causing the plane to crash. Oh well, it wasn't going to be a boring flight.

About thirty minutes after being airborne, a very elderly, stooped-over lady, well into her eighties, in traditional dress who kept walking up and down the aisle, looking carefully at everyone. I assumed she was simply uncomfortable for some health reason. Then after about the fifth walk-by, she stopped at my aisle seat and dropped her passport and the documents needed on arrival in Egypt. She said nothing. I immediately understood. She was looking for someone she knew would be able to fill out the form, and at the same time, would pose no threat. There I was, a young Westerner in a suit and tie, who would not likely try to rob her. I had passed her reliability test. After dutifully filling out the forms, I returned the forms and her passport. She gave me such a warm smile that I can still see her face in front of me today.

After my stay in Lagos, when I arrived in Cairo, I felt like I had just landed in Sweden. I was back to *civilization*. The courtesy of the Egyptians was comforting after the tensions felt in Lagos.

Bond Market Challenges

In 1996, several years after joining Moody's sovereign risk unit, I was promoted to Managing Director. Once I became a Managing Director, my travel became somewhat less exotic. The period between 1992-1996 was filled with new and exciting places to visit. At ITC, I worked behind the scenes, with little or no public persona. At Moody's, which only recently had begun to rate foreign government bonds, after a fifty-year hiatus, everything suddenly became newsworthy. I had to be careful about any public statements about countries or governments.

In those early years, at Moody's, we were told to avoid the spotlight as much as possible. We tried to stay behind the scenes. This didn't work as the rating agency became more important for financial markets and thus for governments. The big change in international markets for EM countries was triggered by the creation of Brady Bonds in 1989. This scheme involved governments of the major creditor countries, the US, in particular, helping to support the rescheduling of sovereign bank debts by allowing the use of their treasury bonds to guarantee final principle payments. These new instruments allowed for the transformation of illiquid bank loans into securities which could be easily traded in the bond markets. It was a means to resolve, not just the sovereign debt problem, but also to help the banks stabilize their capital structures. It's estimated that about $160 billion of bonds of many

EM countries suddenly were trading in international markets.

Prior to the Great Depression, most countries borrowed money in the highly developed international bond market. Once the depression hit, most countries defaulted on their bonds. As a result, the market for foreign currency sovereign bonds disappeared. Even after WW II, there was still no appetite for foreign sovereign bonds. This was a major backdrop for the creation of such international financial institutions, collectively known as IFIs, were created. The two most important were the International Monetary Fund (IMF) and the World Bank. They would be the major suppliers of liquidity for both advanced nations and for EM countries.

IFI funds or bilateral aid, such as the Marshall Plan, remained the major source of international funding. Things only changed in 1973, when the price of oil suddenly quadrupled. It's important to keep in mind some basic international economic principles. Despite what the average person thinks, a trade deficit or a current deficit can only occur if such deficits are financed. This meant that if the oil exporters wished to export oil at the much higher price, that could only occur if importing countries had access to funds to buy that oil.

The major oil exporters had no desire to lend to countries all over the world. Instead, they deposited the export proceeds in the major international banks, in the US, Western Europe and Japan. These banks then could and would lend those funds to countries, which needed them. This allowed for the circulation of petrodollars. Over time, however, this resulted in big increases in foreign currency debt, this time owed to commercial banks. Private sector lending to sovereigns began in earnest for the first time since the pre-Depression period.

Some have said, the history of sovereign lending is the history of sovereign default. Sovereigns have been defaulting for a very long time. The first recorded sovereign debt default occurred in the 4rd century BC, when the Attic Maritime Association in Greece defaulted on the Delos Temple Fund, a major source of capital throughout the Eastern Mediterranean. Following this default, the Temple Fund stopped lending to such sovereign institutions. The Roman Empire defaulted on numerous occasions. Even England defaulted in 1327 under King Edward III. Two Italian banks collapsed as a result.

Between 1500 and 1900, France defaulted on average every thirty years. The French Comptroller General, Joseph Marie Terray, known as the Abbe Terray, was a colorful character. He recommended that every nation should default at least once every one-hundred years in order to *cleanse itself*. He repudiated French government debt, stopped paying interest and demanded new loans even if the creditors didn't want to lend.

In the 1800s, numerous countries in Latin America defaulted, over half of which were in default by 1880. The list of countries in Europe which defaulted before WW I included Austria, Spain, Greece, Portugal, Russia and Turkey. Most of these countries defaulted on numerous occasions. Five German states also defaulted, as did a number of US states prior to the Civil War, including Pennsylvania, Maryland, Mississippi and Louisiana.

In the US, Barings was the main 19th century international banker for the US. Campaign contributions are not new. It is reported that Barings campaigned heavily for two candidates for Governor in Pennsylvania and Maryland, both of whom pledged to repay the debts of their states. Fortunately for Barings, both candidates won and instituted harsh economic policies enabling the repayment of the debt. Of course, the eleven states of the Confederacy defaulted as well as the Confederacy itself.

Yet, we should be happy to see that foreign creditors only tried to influence US politics, because elsewhere, creditor country governments sent in the troops to occupy the country, especially its customs house, a common practice in Latin America. Britain used a default by Egypt as the pretext to create a protectorate there. France went so far as to invade Turkey over defaulted debts.

Prior to WW II, sovereign immunity was absolute. No national government could be sued in a court of law. That meant that private creditors were at a great disadvantage. After WW II, sovereign immunity began to erode, not because creditors demanded it, but because so many companies had been nationalized following WW II. These companies were in legal limbo. Counterparties on any contract worried that contracts with government-owned companies might be exempt from legal disputes. Countries wanted sovereign immunity for their own government-owned companies to be limited, thus allowing those companies to function as would any other company.

Although sovereign immunity laws limited immunity for companies, these laws did not eliminate it for governments. This proved important during both the debt crisis of the 1980s and for sovereign bond defaults starting with Ecuador in 1997.

In the 1980s, it was useless for banks to sue governments over foreign currency debts. It would be many years before any foreign court sided with private creditors over sovereign-related debts. In the 1980s and 1990s, courts interpreted a government's right to limit foreign exchange, even to foreign creditors, as an extension of a country's monetary sovereignty. Legal interpretations are always malleable. This, interpretation would eventually be limited.

Since sovereign lending often results in sovereign default, the key issue for bond markets was how would defaults on international sovereign bonds be treated, and what would be the consequences of a bond default.

Banks are regulated institutions, which are subject to being strong-armed by their home government. The big banks knew they needed to cooperate with their regulator who had an interest in resolving the sovereign debt problem. In addition, big banks wanted to continue to do business in countries that defaulted. This made rescheduling of bank debts difficult, but orderly. Bondholders were different. They had little interest in the impact on a country of a sovereign debt rescheduling. They just wanted to be repaid.

Rescheduling bonds also posed another difficulty. For years, sovereign bonds did not contain any clauses allowing for a supermajority of bondholders to accept a rescheduling. This meant that if only one investor opposed the rescheduling, then the rescheduling wouldn't continue. It was all the more complicated by the fact that almost all international dollar-denominated bonds were subject either to UK or New York State law. Any disputes would be settled in those courts, both of which were completely independent of any political interference. In addition, because of sovereign immunity, sovereign bonds were not subject to any bankruptcy proceeding. This made sovereign bonds riskier than other types of bonds with the same credit profile.

With the sudden growth of an international bond market for EM countries, Moody's wound up in the center of it all, along with Standard & Poor's (S&P), the other major US rating agency. I also should add that Moody's had been changed completely in the 1980s when Tom McGuire joined Moody's from Goldman Sachs, the investment bank.

Credit ratings are a peculiar *animal*. A huge amount of information is supposed to be summarized in a single rating. Over time, modifications were made to the ratings scale, adding notching to produce greater distinctions among the ratings. It wasn't until the 1990s that Moody's eventually added outlooks to ratings in an attempt to provide more nuanced information.

Everything we did in the Sovereign Risk Unit was not just public, it often was often big news. It wouldn't take long after joining Moody's that I learned how sensitive sovereign ratings could be. One of my first assignments was to handle the rating for Australia. I was briefed on the history of the rating and the controversy that surrounded it.

Apparently, several years before, Moody's had downgraded the rating for the Australian Government. As a result, Moody's sovereign analysts were considered *personae non grata*. For a period of time, Moody's sovereign analysts couldn't meet with any Australian officials. Also, the name Moody's had become etched into the Australian psyche. When I arrived in the early 1990s, things had calmed down enough so that I was able to visit Australia, including meeting with government officials. Yet, I still received a sly comment from the immigration officer when he asked why I was in Australia and where I worked. At the beginning, government officials were not very cooperative, but as time passed, the relationship between Moody's and the government normalized.

Today, most people wouldn't even remember the controversy of the 1980s.

During the early 1990s, Italy suffered a series of crises, both political and economic. I was not the lead analyst for Italy, the one in charge of handling the rating process, from analyzing economic and political data, recommending a rating, and bringing that recommendation before a rating committee. I was the back-up analyst, or the one who followed everything related to the rating in case the lead analyst wasn't available to speak with investors, or to replace the lead analyst if that analyst left Moody's. The lead analyst left in 1993, making me the lead analyst for Italy. The country had already been downgraded as the crises kept coming.

It's important to understand how rating decisions were made. Rating outcomes were always made by a simple majority vote of eligible rating committee members. In an attempt to make sure that senior managers would not automatically sway the committee result, which was the common practice at rating committee at banks. Senior managers in banks always seemed to get the result they preferred. That was not true at Moody's

To reduce the risk of excessive influence, voting started with the most junior members of the rating committee, proceeding up to the most senior, usually the managing director. On occasion, in very important country rating committees, higher ranked staff would join the committee. However, senior staff only included people who worked in the ratings area, never coming from the commercial side of the business.

For years, Moody's refused to create a sovereign ratings methodology. Instead there was a special personnel policy adopted for the sovereign team. People were only hired if they had at least ten-years' experience doing sovereign risk or a closely related field. In the early 1990s, there was a pool of such people, including myself, who had worked for banks. This allowed that approach to work.

Moody's avoided hiring people from the IFIs, such as the IMF or World Bank because we thought they would be too academically oriented, and not have enough background in real-time markets.

Given the breadth of knowledge within the team, it was felt that it was better to just have this incredible group of people debate the pros and cons of economic and political issues related to the government and country under discussion. It was as close to an academic atmosphere as could be found on Wall Street. The aim was to reduce arbitrage within financial markets. Our goal was to provide additional information, allowing investors to make more informed investment decisions. Our ratings were never investment recommendations. Ratings were an informed opinion about credit risk, and credit risk alone.

To guarantee that there would be a constant flow of new viewpoints, we had another special rule within the team.

No one was promoted from within the team. Junior people, who were not allowed to vote on rating committees, were expected to work in the sovereign risk unit for several years and then move onto another position outside Moody's. For years, the problem was that these junior staff members didn't often leave. They enjoyed what they were doing, so they stayed, even if at the time, it was technically a *dead-end job*.

This policy eventually had to change for one important reason. As time passed, there were fewer and fewer available sovereign analysts with bank experience. Commercial banks had gotten out of sovereign lending in the early 1990s, so they no longer needed large teams of sovereign analysts. We then began to allow *junior* staff members to be promoted to analyst, allowing them to become lead analysts and to vote on rating committees. I use the word *junior* with caution, since most of them had years of experience working in the field alongside the senior analysts.

When John Rutherfurd became CEO, he told me that he had been warned by his predecessor, Bill Dwyer, to never attend a sovereign rating committee. Mr. Dwyer had attended one during his tenure simply to see how sovereign committees worked. He said the rating committee was unlike any other rating committee he had ever sat in on before. There were robust arguments, with lots of cross-talk. He said it was *chaos*. What he really witnessed was a group of people who worked together like a *well-oiled machine* where members understood each other so well that they could almost anticipate what the other would say. The raucousness didn't disappear for many years.

For years, David Levey and I co-headed the sovereign risk unit. We rarely agreed on anything, but I think I can confidently say that we both respected and liked each other. Our disagreements were simply intellectual disputes. David had a reputation for being optimistic. We called him *Mr. Sunshine*, even to his face. I was far more cautious, worrying about everything that could go wrong in a country. I'm sure there must have been a nickname for me within the group, but if there was, I never heard it.

The debates David and I had during rating committees were labelled, by some, as *The David and Vincent Show*, because people thought it reminded them of political debates by TV pundits on opposing sides of an argument.

Italy in Crisis

Becoming lead analyst for Italy in 1993 began my *baptism-by-fire*. As background, the Italian economy did relatively well during the 1980s. By the early 1990s, by some measures, Italian GDP had surpassed French GDP. This was not to last long.

High domestic and foreign debt had grown to extremely high levels. The economy was in the midst of selling-off state-owned-enterprises (SOEs). Italian civil society was not, and still is not able to deal with radical reform such as that undertaken by a left-wing German government by passing the so-called Hartz Reforms, which fundamentally changed German labor laws. Italy has been and is still capable of instituting economic and political reforms, but the reforms need to be more gradual if they are going to work.

In 1979, the EEC, the predecessor of the EU, had adopted the Exchange Rate Mechanism (ERM). After WW II, fixed exchange rates dominated the international financial system. The US dollar, along with gold, stood at the center of the entire international monetary system. Between 1933-1971, Americans were not allowed to own gold, except for gold jewelry. Gold for US jewelry was sold at $90/oz. At the same time, foreign holdings of dollars were exchangeable into gold at $35/oz (government transactions, not individual transactions). This difference in the price of gold explains why most US jewelry, for decades, has been 14K gold, not the 18K variety popular elsewhere. Before drugs became a major problem, customs officials would primarily be looking for the *illegal* importation of gold. The arbitrage was huge: $90/oz vs. $35/oz.

By 1971, it had become clear that the US gold standard, upon which the international financial system was based, was no longer tenable. On August 15, 1971, President Nixon announced the US dollar would no longer be tied to gold. The Bretton Woods fixed-exchange rate system was dead. At the same time, there was great resistance to flexible exchange rates. That resistance to flexible exchange rates explains the 1979 ERM agreement.

The ERM allowed exchange rates of member states to vary within two narrow ranges of either 2.25 or 6 percent, depending on the economic needs of the member states. All of this was being done in preparation for an eventual monetary union of EEC member states.

Italy had often used changes in its exchange rate to compensate for its lack of competitiveness resulting from its rigid market mechanisms. When rigidities caused too much loss of competitiveness, a devaluation would take place, and the process would begin again.

Foolishly, the UK joined the ERM in 1990. However, sterling exchange rate was under enormous downward pressure by September 1992, forcing the UK to leave the ERM. A few days before the British withdrawal, Italy had devalued the lira. With the British withdrawal from the

ERM following the recent Italian devaluation caused markets to expect Italy might be next. To avoid leaving the ERM completely, Italy allowed the lira to float within the ERM, with the expectation that it would eventually return to the ERM.

With a high debt and now with a flexible exchange rate for the first time, Italian markets were under enormous stress. At the same time, Italy was in political crisis for somewhat different reasons. There was the killing of two anti-Mafia magistrates. The first killing took place in May. The second magistrate was killed in July, in a bomb blast using over killing of the prosecutor using about 200 pounds of a plastic explosive. The devastation caused by the blast shocked the country. This caused the central government to send in the military, at one point reaching 150,000 soldiers, to occupy Sicily for about six years.

If this wasn't bad enough, in Milan, magistrates were investigating corruption on a grand scale. Under the banner of *Tangentopoli* (*Bribesville*), political corruption was found to be widespread, reaching the highest levels of the political class.

To make matters more complicated, national elections took place. Everything was in flux, because this was Italy's first election without a large Communist Party. The party had disbanded following the collapse of the Soviet Union. It also represents the emergence of the Northern League, a party dedicated to ending domination by the central government. They even called for Italy's North to become independent.

I was thrown into this morass. I had been following developments in Italy as backup analyst. In late February 1993, I called for a rating committee, where we decided to put Italy's ratings under review for downgrade. The announcement was explosive. That day, the President of Italy said that Moody's was part of an international conspiracy to destabilize the country. Moody's was once again at the center of a storm.

WTC Terror Attack 1993 and *Dietrologia*

I will always remember the day we put Italy on review for downgrade. The following day, I had a dentist appointment in Battery Park City, not far from Moody's. It was around lunchtime, when I started walking back to the office. It was snowing lightly, so instead of walking above ground, I decided to go through the underground network of tunnels, which connect me to the 99 Church Street office. There was a walkway crossing West Street. On the other side of the walkway, there was an escalator down to World Trade Center shopping mall. As soon as I opened the doors to enter the shopping mall, there was a huge explosion. The force of the explosion pushed me from head to toe. All I could then hear was the slamming shut of the metal gates in front of the stores. The sound was deafening. I knew immediately that it had been some sort of terrorist attack. I ran in the direction that the wind was pushing me. I soon passed the massive bank of escalators which led to the New Jersey Path trains. Gray smoke was billowing up the escalators. People were crawling up the escalators as quickly as they could. Within a few minutes, I reached the entrance of Moody's.

Arriving at my office, I was breathless from the experience. It was immediately obvious that it as terrorism. My colleagues, half-jokingly, then said that the Italian President was just getting even with me for the rating review. Although, the Italian government wasn't responsible for the WTC bombing, it was the first instance where Italian conspiracy theories came to the fore. It seemed like nothing in Italy could ever be what it appeared to be. There always had to be something unknown behind it. In Italian, there is a word to describe this phenomenon: *dietrologia*. Conspiracy theories were not limited to Italy. As I will discuss later, the Japanese are particularly fond of it, too. In the 1990s, in the US, conspiracy theories were few-and-far between, reserved to a small group of people with extremist views. In recent years, that has changed. We should now borrow the Italian word to describe the American obsession with conspiracies.

A trip to Italy was soon organized by Goldman Sachs. We would meet with Italian officials in the Treasury, the Central Bank, along with the most senior politicians. In addition, we met with well-known academics as well as businessmen and even labor union leaders. This was a far cry from my solo ITC visits to countries.

One of the most interesting meetings actually involved a dinner at a senior official's home. Around the table was a small group, about ten or twelve men, who represented a *Who's Who* of Italian politics and finance.

Italian politics had become so dysfunctional, that as many as one-third of the Parliament was under indictment for some sort of crime, largely tied to Tangentopoli. It reached a point where it had become impossible to form a political government. Instead, a technocratic government was formed. Instead of being a member of parliament, the head of the Bank of Italy, Carlo Azeglio Ciampi, was named Prime Minister. The Bank of Italy was the only government institution that was well respected by Italians and foreigners alike.

Most senior politicians and finance leaders, we met with, apologized for the Italian President's accusation that Moody's was part of international conspiracy. They said that he didn't fully understand how the financial system operated.

That trip was also a lesson for me in how high-level Moody's issuer trips were to be handled. Tom McGuire accompanied me and others on the trip because of the importance and visibility of the rating. This was unusual. As previously noted, Tom McGuire basically invented the modern ratings industry framework. He often repeated that he wanted us to concentrate only on the narrow focus of the rating. We prided ourselves, at the time, on being a flat organization, with little or no hierarchy. (I doubt that's true today.)

He told me to introduce him as *a colleague from New York*. No titles were given for anyone. The Goldman Sachs people certainly knew, as well as many senior Italian officials, that Tom McGuire was a very important man within Moody's. Since he was a master of manipulation, this must have put the Italians off-guard, likely asking themselves, "Why is he doing that?" Brilliant!

One of the *funniest* or *worst* cartoons produced as a result of the Italian rating was published by the International Financial Review (IFR). In it was a man who looked quite like David Levey, including his iconic eyeglasses. He was then the sole Managing Director of the unit. In the cartoon, he was getting out of a bed, which had a severed horse's head dripping in blood, an obvious reference to the *Godfather* movie. This just proved to be the just the beginning of hilarious, satirical cartoons about Moody's sovereign team rating actions.

The end result of that trip was a downgrade of the Italian rating. Markets were riled. I had to follow events in Italy very closely, first as the lead analyst, then beginning in 1996, as Managing Director, and along with David Levey, Co-Head of the unit.

I often traveled to Italy, not just to meet with officials, politicians and academics, but I was also frequently asked to give speeches regarding the economy and the rating.

One memorable trip was to Palermo, where I spoke at a conference. What was special was not just the attendees, but the location. It was held at the Grand Hotel Villa Igiea on the Palermo coast. It was restored in the 19th century and was one of those great hotels built or renovated to provide accommodations for wealthy British on their *Grand Tour*. These hotels are distinctive in that there is a heavy use of wood, something not commonly used in Italy, but which made British tourists feel more like home. Everything about the hotel was spectacular. The main rooms, the dining rooms, even the hallways brought you back to the 19th century. In addition, there was lots of art, including many ancient Roman and Greek statues in the gardens. My room was large, with a balcony set high on a cliff overlooking the Mediterranean. To make it unrivaled to any hotel I have ever stayed at, that night there was a full moon, visible from the balcony, with the moonlight shimmering on the dark, shining Mediterranean. Unbelievably romantic!

Once I was a Managing Director, I increasingly gave speeches or presentations. On one trip to Milan, I was invited to La Scala, one of the world's great opera houses. I enjoyed sitting in one of the opera boxes, which was unlike most others I have seen in other opera houses around the world. The boxes were truly intimate. I could easily imagine lovers going furtively back and forth between these boxes. It was all great fun.

After the opera, it was late, and the streets were quiet. One of the conference attendees was staying at the same hotel I was. With pleasant weather and a desire to walk off some of the food we had eaten earlier at another large dinner, we decided to walk back to the hotel. We had a fascinating conversation about emerging markets. He had incredible travel stories because he visited companies he was interested in, which usually were off-the-beaten path. At the time, I confess I didn't know who he was. I later learned that I had been walking with one the legends of emerging market or frontier investors, Mark Mobius. That night, he provided me with insights that proved quite useful over the years. I'm sure he would not likely remember me or that walk.

On another trip to Italy, following a major crisis in the Italian bond market, I met with some investment bankers that I had known for years. There was a growing problem with treasury bond auctions. Some of them were failing, which may have presaged a major crisis. However, I was told that the crisis was dealt with by the Bank of Italy instructing the country's big banks to buy the treasury bonds, which the central bank would immediately rediscount. It was a brilliant scheme. It surreptitiously got around one of the Maastricht rules about central banks financing deficits. This allowed the central bank to deny it was funding the government directly, which would have contravened Maastricht, even though it arranged everything to mimic that result. This is a good example of the difference between the *letter-of-the-law* and the *spirit-of-the-law*. International finance is complicated, where not everything is as it seems. Perhaps, Dietrologia is not such a strange concept.

China

I was also the lead analyst for China. As I have already written, I had studied Mandarin in high school. I took courses in East Asian history in college. I had followed developments in China for decades out of personal interest.

On my first trip to China, the rating team, once again, included Tom McGuire. The reason was similar to the Italian trip; this was a very visible and important rating. The rest of the team consisted of David Levey and Jonathan Schiffer. As usual, Moody's operated differently from S&P, sometimes in very strange ways.

The Chinese government offered for us to stay at their famous foreign guest houses, located in a beautiful park-like section in Beijing. The mansions laid out in an idyllic setting. Tom McGuire said, no. We couldn't stay there because he didn't want the Chinese government to provide us free accommodation, which he considered a conflict of interest. Therefore, we stayed at a very nice Beijing hotel. However, the meetings still took place at one of the guest houses. We were picked up daily and driven in two separate limousines. We even had a police escort with sirens blazing. Another WOW moment!

I had heard from knowledgeable sources that the government preferred for us to stay in the guest houses because there we would have been *comforted* by the beautiful female staff. I have no idea if that was true, but it sounded good enough for me to believe.

On the first few visits to China, first as lead analyst, and then as Managing Director, were not very valuable for information-gathering purposes. It was odd that even if the official spoke fluent English, he was not permitted to speak English at the meetings. Everything had to be translated by official translators. I assumed that this was done to restrict open communication. If the official said anything *awkward* the translator could *fix* that. Anyway, it made these official meetings even longer and more boring than necessary.

The really important parts of the first trip centered around the meals. I have to confess that this was my first experience with a formal Chinese banquet, which as you may know, is quite different from the Chinese food that was served in the West, at least before more recent Chinese immigration changed our culinary knowledge of Chinese regional cuisines.

I had expected to see rice served at our formal dinners. However, no rice was served. When I asked about it, I was told that rice was considered too common; another sign that we were being treated with the utmost respect. Although I like Chinese cuisine, there are some things that I refuse to eat, one of which is sea urchin. When it would arrive, and it always did, I would simply feign eating it, playing around with it using my chopsticks. Since there were so many courses, I don't think anyone noticed.

I was treated as the guest of honor, despite Tom McGuire being part of the team. At formal Chinese banquets, seating order is extremely important, as it is in the West. The guest of honor would sit next to the host. Others would be seated by order of their rank. Although Tom McGuire and David Levey technically out-ranked me, they were seated on the far side of the circular table. Perhaps Tom's penchant for indicating that he was *just a colleague*, influenced the Chinese seating order.

I dislike most fish. However, one of the fanciest foods at such a banquet was a large fish that was roasted and presented with its mouth and eyes wide open. As the guest of honor, I was given the first opportunity to take some of the fish. I was told by my hosts that the best part was near the mouth and gills. I dutifully took from the part of the fish I was told was for me. I forced myself to eat it. It was the polite and necessary thing to do. To be honest, it wasn't that bad. In fact, for fish eaters, it was probably very tasty. It was just wasted on me.

The most interesting parts of the meals, as is true everywhere in the world, were the individual conversations around the table. The most incredible conversation I had was with a very senior official, who shall remain unnamed. I mean really senior!

I soon found that the Chinese are obsessed with ethnic backgrounds. He leaned over to me and asked, "What is your family background?"

I responded that I was Italian-American, and that my family had emigrated from Italy about one hundred years ago. The he said, "Ahhh, you are from an old and ancient culture, not like these barbarians!" waving his arm as he pointed to my colleagues. This was certainly a side of China I had not yet seen. Over time, I would find that the Chinese are quite racist, at least they are no different from anyone else in the world. I have found racism across the globe. There always seems to be a hierarchy of ethnic groups, which simply vary from region to region.

A colleague, who had taught for several years at a university in Hong Kong, told me that often when he would sit in a subway car, ethnic Chinese people would often change their seat. I later learned that Westerners often smell unpleasant to East Asians because of the large quantity of dairy products we consume.

In my early years at Moody's, I flew first class to East Asia. I used Singapore Airlines many times. It had, by far, the best first-class service I had ever seen. What's relevant here is that on these incredibly long flights, you got to know the stewardesses. I was joking about what I had heard about Westerners and dairy products to two of them. They then told me that they had to be trained to eat Western cheeses, by sampling some, because for them, it was such an unpleasant food, yet it was a main staple of high-end meals they served on-board. Then I thought about all the cheeses I love, but which have a terrible smell. I guess familiarity allows me to ignore the funky smells of those cheeses.

The trips to China became more informative over time. They became less formal. The most incredible meeting I ever had with any Chinese officials was when I met with a group from the Bank of China. As usual, the Chinese officials sat opposite us, with the most senior person in the center, facing directly across from me.

We began to discuss the usual monetary policy issues. At the time, the central bank was using what they labeled *unorthodox policy measures*. The central bank was putting strict credit limits on bank branches. I had heard that these credit limits were often breached. I asked the gentleman in the center of the Chinese bank team, how were local branches able to breach the credit restrictions? His response was one of the most forthright explanations I ever heard from anyone on almost any sovereign risk trip.

Smiling, he said there were many tools at the disposal of local governments to influence local bank branches. One measure was to shut off the electricity to the branch. All the other officials smiled and shook their heads in agreement. Then he said, sometimes the water would be cut off. Again, there were more broad smiles and head-nodding. He then said that if the branch manager would still not be cooperative, the local government might throw his children and those of his staff out of their schools. That response got the most enthusiastic smiles and head-nodding across the table. What could I say? Chinese banking functioned quite differently from what we were used to seeing. At the same time, from frankness like this, I slowly began to take what Chinese officials said more seriously than before. Chinese officials used disinformation far less than almost any other EM government I would meet with.

Government Disinformation

The best anecdote about government use of disinformation came to light long after the fact. On a trip to the umpteenth conference where I would speak, somewhere in Europe, I met a Spanish investment banker. He asked if I recognized him. I said he looked familiar, but honestly, I couldn't immediately place him. He then said that he had been the Spanish official in charge of liaising with the rating agencies. He followed with this question, "Did you know what my real job was?" I thought he was going to say something about some mundane tasks he had. Instead, he replied, "My main job was to lie to the rating agencies!" A surprise, but not a surprise. It was further proof of what we always suspected.

The mid-1990s was a wild period for me. Handling Italy, China, Australia seemed burden enough. However, I had a number of other countries to follow, the most exciting turned out to be Canada. Since I had studied for years in Montreal, and spoke French, I seemed like the obvious candidate.

Canada

At that time, Canadian provinces and local governments were included in the Public Finance team, which was responsible for rating US states and US local governments. It may seem foolish today, but in the mid-to-late 90s, there was extreme competition between public finance and the fundamental or corporate and sovereign ratings group. It had little to do with analytics. It centered around internal power politics, with Tom McGuire on one side and the head of public finance on the other. These tensions lasted for years, until the board of directors finally resolved it.

One important member of the Canadian ratings team was Yves Lemay, a pleasant guy from Quebec, who had previously worked in the Canadian Ministry of Finance. This is relevant because public finance had a different relationship to issuers from the fundamental side. Public finance staff were close to their issuers. They were openly friendly. They often went to dinner with them. This was not allowed on the fundamental side. The more standoffish we were, the better.

S&P was known as *statistical*, while Moody's was known as *mystical*. Our press releases might have been written by the Delphic Oracle. It was intentional. It gave a special aura to the ratings, which were only recently becoming an important part of the financial system.

I remember Tom McGuire saying that the only reason Moody's had sovereign ratings was because of the reputational spillover effect, or as he termed it, *the halo effect*. He turned out to be quite right.

Given that any change in the Canadian rating would immediately affect local Canadian provincial and municipal ratings, the sovereign team and the public finance team, both of which had very different cultures had to work together.

One result of this difference in corporate cultures was that the sovereign team avoided the press whenever possible. Public finance didn't mind speaking with reporters. Eventually, as a result of the Canadian rating challenge, the fundamental group made some important changes to our modus operandi moving closer to friendliness and transparency.

Canada was in serious economic, financial and political difficulties in the mid-1990s. The Federal Government as well as many provinces had large debts and out-of-control spending. Added to this witches' brew was the issue of Quebec, something that has swirled throughout Canadian history.

Throughout these years, what was often lost on most people was that we were talking about a Aaa rating for Canada. Even a downgrade meant the risk of default was still extremely low. However, as I have observed around the world, sovereign ratings are often viewed as a kind of country beauty contest. At the upper levels of the rating scale, default risk is nearly impossible to distinguish.

Ratings are, by their very nature, ordinal. It was only after decades of recording defaults against the various ratings on defaulted issuers, that there was ever an attempt to associate a rating with any specific cardinal default risk. None of this matters in the court of public opinion.

Given that ratings are considered status symbols by most governments, in most countries that are downgraded, or put on review for downgrade, citizens usually oppose that move. Such was the case in Australia in the 1980s. Of all countries, which were put on review for downgrade, and/or were downgraded, the Canadian reaction was totally different. I would get calls and emails from average Canadians saying that their country should be downgraded. This is a question for Canadian sociologists to explore. I never could figure it out.

Moody's had only recently opened an office in Toronto. Hillary Parkes and her small staff bore the brunt of the reporting frenzy that developed resulting from putting the Canadian Aaa rating on review for downgrade. She and her staff had to barricade the doors to keep out the reporters demanding interviews.

When the rating team arrived in Canada, out first stop was Ottawa. This time, the team didn't include Tom McGuire, but instead Ken Pinkes, Tom's second-incommand, one of the smartest men I have ever known. I am sure he would blush if he ever reads this. The meetings in Ottawa went without incident. I remember the Finance Minister having lunch with us. It was a far cry from what we were served in Italy and China.

We simply sat down at a table in a conference room, where we had sandwiches. It was exactly what Moody's would serve for lunch when issuers or investors met with us at our head-office. I have to confess that dealing with Canadian officials was always a pleasure. At the same time, when the rating review was concluded, we called the Finance Ministry telling officials that we were downgrading the Canadian rating. It was about one or two hours before the announcement. Then we got a huge surprise. Soon after the public release of the rating, many market participants complained to us that Canadian Crown corporations (SOEs) had gone into the FX market and made a bundle on the exchange rate fall. This was unbelievable. The government had used this information to make money off its own investors. Such insider trading would be illegal in both the US and Canada, but, because it involved the government, nothing ever came of it. Moody's from then on, never provided a rating outcome to a government with more than 30-45 minutes. Our aim was always to reduce arbitrage, not increase it. Today, regulations now require governments receive the rating decision well in advance of any public announcement, which I believe is one of the dumber ideas regulators could have come up with. It's of no help to market participants, and only exists to make politicians happy. I am sure almost no one knew that a government such a Canada did what it did in 1994. Imagine what EM countries now do with that knowledge. I assume lots of government officials and their families have made lots of money using this inside information to game a rating change.

I was inundated with calls from reporters starting with the review for downgrade, and for a long time afterwards. Moody's policy remained to avoid the press if possible. I believe that there were no TV interviews or in-person interviews with reporters immediately following the rating action. It didn't quiet down for Hillary and her staff. They were at the center of a political storm.

Canadian Prime Minister Jean Chretien complained openly about 28-year-old currency traders in New York, wearing red suspenders who could quickly wreck Canada's economy. As reported later, Canadian officials at the following G-7 meeting were happy that Italy's crisis appeared worse than Canada's. They were relieved that Canada was the second worst, not *the* worst.

I remember at one investor meeting we held in Toronto, where it got so raucous that I had to hide for a time in the men's room. TV reporters kept trying to interview me.

Avoiding press contact caused some humorous results. The best was a two-page article in the Toronto Star, with the headline, **What Color Are Vincent Truglia's Eyes?** In it were interviews with well-known Canadians who had met me in person. Some told the reporter, it was an irrelevant question. I don't remember if anyone actually indicated that my eyes are brown. The coup de grace was at the end, when the reporter said that I was more famous and more important than Madonna, who was then at the peak of her career.

As the years passed, when provincial premiers visited Moody's, and when I would first meet them, a number of them would lean across the conference room table and say, "I see your eyes are brown!" or something similar. It often broke the ice.

I wrote a special comment trying to point out the exaggerated risk investors were interpreting by a downgrade at such a high rating. Nothing mattered. After reading about some of my comments, a Canadian author, Linda McQuaig asked to interview me in my office for a book she was writing. She wasn't writing a newspaper story, but a book, so it seemed like that would be useful for everyone.

When her book, *Shooting the Hippo: Death by Deficit and Other Canadian Myths*, finally came out, I was surprised, and that's putting it mildly. Most of the chapter was dedicated to our meeting with the provocative chapter heading *Scissorhands Meets the Deficit Slayer*. Although, her description of me and my supposed power was a bit over-the-top, her fundamental interpretation of what I had told her was correct. Canadians and bond markets were exaggerating the risk of Canada defaulting on its Federal government debt.

US Immigration and Newark

On one of my many trips to Canada, this time to give some briefings in Toronto, I flew there, knowing I could return the same day. No need for a hotel. That proved to be a problem, because I always kept my passport in my carry-on bag. This trip didn't require any carry-on bags, meaning when I arrived at the airport in New York, I didn't have my passport to show at check-in. This was pre-9/11, when security was tight, but still lax compared to today.

I knew you didn't need a passport if you drove across the border. At that time, you only were required to have to take a flight to Canada. I was told that the airline could not guarantee that Canadian immigration would allow me into the country. I said, that's not a problem. I had lived in Canada and thought I would easily gain entry. On arrival in Toronto, after giving my sob story about forgetting my passport to the immigration agent I was let in.

After my briefings, I went back to the airport to return home. For those who are not familiar with how customs and immigration to the US works when flying from Canada to the US, the US maintains customs and immigration officers at the largest Canadian airports such as Toronto and Montreal. Once again, I repeated my tale of woe about forgetting my passport.

The US immigration officer looked me up and down and asked, "Where were you born?" I responded, "Newark, New Jersey." She then said, "No one would lie about that!" I was allowed to return to the US without further incident. Newark's reputation in those days was not good, and that's putting it mildly.

At a meeting with the Canadian Finance Minister, Paul Martin, he told me that in retrospect, he was grateful for the downgrade. It made it far easier for him to fix Canada's deficit problem. He indicated that at cabinet meetings the Prime Minister shot down any ministerial requests for more money. Given Jean Chretien's reputation for being a no-nonsense man, ministers understood that he wouldn't give in to their requests. The result: large cuts in government spending, especially a reduction in the size Canada's welfare state. There were only small tax increases. The result was a quick turnaround in the Federal government deficit. Federal government debt/GDP ratio peaked in 1996, and then declined and continued to decline, for the next twelve years, through 2008, the beginning of the Great Recession.

Quebec

Not just economics and finances were in crisis in the mid-1990s. The Federal government also faced the real possibility that Quebec might leave the Federation.

The idea of independence for the province became more important during the post-WW II period, following the so-called *Quiet Revolution*.

The province had remained a conservative bastion of pre-Vatican II Roman Catholicism, dating back to the British conquest in 1759.

After winning the *French and Indian War,* the British found themselves governing a large group of ethnic French. In a brilliant tactical move, the British allowed the Quebecois to keep their religion, and to maintain their culture without interference. Over time, most anglophones concentrated themselves in urban areas such as Montreal and Quebec City. Francophones overwhelmingly populated rural areas.

By the mid-20th century, as francophones became better educated, they increasingly moved to Quebec's cities. This mass urbanization changed how francophones viewed their traditions. They were proud of their francophone culture, but now saw it through a modern lens, setting the stage for *The Quiet Revolution*. Everything was changing. Francophones demanded more say in the economic system. This translated into demanding more equal rights for francophones in the workplace. This was the force behind Quebec's language laws beginning in the 1970s, which made French the dominant language throughout the public domain. These laws went so far as to ban the use of English on signs and storefronts. Laws changed, requiring immigrants to go French language schools.

Access to English language schools became severely restricted.

The 1980s was a period of consolidation of the *francophonization* of the province. In response to growing calls for more autonomy for Quebec, Prime Minister Elliot Trudeau began the process of patriation of the Canadian Constitution, which until then had been subject to formal approval by the UK parliament, through amendments to the British North America Act. It had to be labeled a *patriation*, rather than a *repatriation* because Canada never had had its own constitution,

All the provinces approved the new constitution, except for Quebec. Battle lines at the Federal level were being drawn. A former federal minister, Lucien Bouchard formed a new federal political party, the *Bloc Quebecois*.

In elections called in 1993, the Bloc won enough seats in parliament to become the official opposition. That gave the Bloc enormous power to politically outmaneuver the Federal government. The Parti Quebecois led the provincial National Assembly. In February 1995, the PQ government called for a second referendum on independence. Here Canada was sitting on a growing debt burden, with the increasing possibility that the country's second largest province, along with its second largest city, might leave the Canadian Federation.

Support for the referendum was aided by on-going Federal budgetary woes. The referendum occurred on

October 30, 1995. The results were incredibly close. Although francophones voted *Yes* vote by margins above 60 percent, anglophones and allophones voted against the referendum by 95 percent.

The *Yes* vote won 49.4 percent of the vote against 50.6 percent for *No*. The *Yes* vote lost by a mere 54,288 votes out of 4,671,008 votes cast. Canada had just dodged a bullet, but only barely.

Despite the closeness of the result, the Federal government was then able to concentrate its energies on fixing its finances, without the referendum distraction.

Throughout the 1990s, it seemed as though crises were occurring more frequently, with shorter intervals between them.

The Tequila Crisis

In 1994, I was not the lead analyst handling Mexico. However, I did sit on several Mexican rating committees. I can't add any personal anecdotes surrounding that rating. However, I believe it is still worth discussing because it had implications far beyond Mexico.

In 1994, Mexico faced a number of challenges. Mexican banks, which had been nationalized in 1982, were privatized in the early 1990s. This led to a credit boom, which is usually risky for any country. Capital controls were removed. The country was regularly running current account deficits. These deficits were then largely financed by short-term portfolio flows. The government used a crawling peg exchange rate mechanism. This allowed a slow and steady depreciation of the peso. There was political unrest in Chiapas in southern Mexico. To make matters worse, the US Federal Reserve had begun to raise interest rates.

As the year progressed, investors believed that the risk was growing of a major peso devaluation. By the end of the year, given the large capital outflows, a devaluation became inevitable. On December 16, $855 million left Mexico in a single day. On December 20-21, $4.6 billion left, or about half the country's international reserves. On December 22, the peso was allowed to float freely, and fell a whopping 35 percent against the dollar before the end of the year.

The Mexican government indicated it cannot meet all its obligations on a timely basis without help. The only other option was to default. The US put together a huge program for Mexico totaling about $50 billion. The program consists of large contributions from the IMF, the BIS, private creditors and $20 billion directly from the US through the Exchange Stabilization Fund, a little-known source of liquidity controlled by the US Treasury.

This allowed the Mexican government to avoid defaulting on its debt. Soon after, the Mexican government put in place a strict austerity program. The new policy framework was viewed favorably by the investment community. Although most commentators discuss the economic and financial impact of the crisis on Mexico, they often leave out the most important long-term political changes that resulted from the crisis.

President Zedillo began a process of democratization that has continued unabated for decades. Before Zedillo, Mexico was widely recognized as an authoritarian, one-party state. With major changes to its electoral laws, Mexico is now definitely a modern, functioning democracy. It's far from perfect, but no government is. When Zedillo left office, he had been so disgraced, including accusations about his brother, that he left Mexico and moved to Ireland for a number of years. His retirement proved quite different from past presidential retirements.

About a year after the Mexican crisis, I met with a finance minister of a small Western democracy, who I had gotten to know well over the years. He had just returned from Beijing. He said Chinese officials told him they were going to reduce the country's short-term debt as soon as possible. They said China was not going to be subjected to political pressure to reform as Mexico was experiencing because of its international financial crisis. His report turned out to be quite accurate. China soon drove down its short-term foreign currency debt. This was coupled with a change in China's foreign exchange regime, which happened at the height of the Peso crisis. China abolished unified its exchange rate regime, implying a depreciation that proved significant enough to make China very competitive compared to other East Asian countries. The period 1994-1995 represents the beginning of China's accumulation of massive international reserves. I doubt most people realized the connection between China's actions and Mexican politics. I certainly wouldn't have without my conversation with a friendly finance minister.

Financial crises were coming with greater frequency and with greater amplitudes. Soon after the Mexican peso crisis, we witnessed the early signs of a crisis in Thailand. I became a Managing Director in 1996. I had been the lead analyst for Thailand before my promotion. What was beginning to become worrisome was the growing difficulty in interpreting Thai statistics, especially those regarding how the government was reporting intercompany loans between Japanese subs and their home offices.

East Asian Crisis

As background for the East Asian crisis, there are a number of overall arching themes. Outside Japan, East Asian nations were growing fairly well for most of the early 1990s. Yet, for some countries, the structure of that growth was changing. For Thailand, Indonesia, and Malaysia, growth was no longer the result of rapid export growth, but growth in real estate investment and increases in non-tradable goods. Domestic investment was being increasingly financed by large private sector capital inflows. Then a number of factors combined and changed the economic playbook.

With a low interest rate environment, the US economy had been growing in the early part of the decade. By mid-decade, US rates were rising in an effort to stem inflationary pressures. Higher US rates made US financial investments more attractive.

The Japanese economy was stagnating as a result of the 1985 Plaza Accord, which caused a sharp appreciation of the yen against other major currencies. To this day, the Japanese economy has never really fully recovered from that agreement.

With weakness in the economy, Japanese banks were under enormous pressure as bad loans mounted. Japanese banks started to retreat from Southeast Asia in an effort to shore-up their balance sheets. With fixed or nearly-fixed exchange rate regimes, most Southeast Asian countries had over-valued FX rates. This made foreign borrowing *seem* cheap. Declining international competitiveness due to overvalued FX rates, caused more investment to be directed to domestic markets. Shopping malls and expensive housing became the *investments-du-jour.*

As Japanese banks retreated, and as US interest rates rose, capital inflows to the region faced ever-shortening maturities. By 1997, a significant portion of foreign-currency debt for Southeast Asian countries was short-term. All that would be needed for a full-blown crisis would be if one of the currencies with a fixed FX rate were to cave and allow that currency to float. Once that would happen, contagion was inevitable, because most of the countries, despite their differences, shared many commonalities.

Thailand

For Thailand, the issue was, were those Japanese inter-company loans truly short-term debts, or were they simply booked that way for internal accounting purposes? I came to the more conservative conclusion and considered them short-term debt. The new lead analyst was extremely cautious, but in a different way. She was more willing to accept Thai assurances that these debts were booked that way only for accounting purposes. Matters were coming to a head. A rating committee decided to put Thailand's rating on review for downgrade by a slim margin.

What happened next, in retrospect, was decisive in blunting the warning the rating committee intended to send the Thai government and investors. It was the only time I ever saw a sovereign analyst go to senior management to protest a rating committee outcome. That was perfectly acceptable, but it proved reckless.

There were only two occasions during my tenure at Moody's that senior management interfered with a valid rating committee outcome. Thailand was the first.

Senior management decided to expand the rating committee to include more people. It was a contentious meeting. In the end, the expanded committee voted to only put the short-term rating of Thailand on review for downgrade. Just reviewing the short-term rating didn't send a strong enough signal to the market, making the review pretty useless as a warning. I wonder to this day, could the East Asian crisis have been avoided or at least made less severe, if the original committee decision had been left standing? We'll never know.

Developments in Thailand kept deteriorating. It wasn't until the following February that the long-term A2 rating was put on review for downgrade. Developments in Thailand demonstrated the need for our bank analysts for the country in question to participate in all sovereign rating committees going forward, a practice we continued from then on.

Concerns were growing steadily throughout 1997. Thailand had maintained a fixed exchange rate for decades. That was causing Thailand's external accounts to deteriorate. In retrospect, I believe the Chinese unification of its exchange rate in 1994, which was the equivalent to a devaluation, making Chinese exports far more competitive than before as the fundamental cause of Thailand's crisis. Thailand was now facing strong Chinese competition in all its export markets.

In May 1997, a major attack on the baht exchange rate took place. The situation was growing worse. However, when we looked at it, the country still had a significant level of international reserves. Then in July, all hell broke loose, when the exchange rate was allowed to float. It turned out that the central bank had been using the forward foreign exchange rate market to dampen speculation. The problem with this was that, although countries such as Italy and the UK have used similar tools during periods of crisis, an EM country like Thailand wasn't capable of undertaking the same actions without producing far different results.

In developed countries, the worse risk a government would face in intervening in the forward market would be a small loss in domestic currency, which would affect the country's budget. The reason was that there were always market participants who would want to buy the local currency. Why? Because of the depth of an advanced economy; there's always something valuable to purchase in those markets. In the case of an EM country, using the forward markets can be risky because market participants might not be willing to acquire any additional local currency, such as the baht.

When it became clear that the central bank had intervened heavily to avoid pressure on the FX rate, and that it would have to sell dollars to complete the contracts, it was obvious that international reserves were massively *overstated*. In other words, although the country still had dollar assets, those assets were required to meet contracts which would come due over time.

As we saw in Mexico, when the exchange rate floated, and depreciated a great deal, domestic banks and other domestic corporations were suddenly saddled with lots of much more expensive foreign currency debt. The Thai economy was in for a terrible period of economic dislocation.

The Thai rating kept falling in both December and January. The rating fell to B2 on January 9. It was obvious that the Moody's team needed to go to Thailand prior to the downgrades. It was the longest short trip I ever made. I flew to Bangkok and returned to New York all within a 53-hour period. I spent less than a day in Thailand. For flight scheduling reasons, I had to circumnavigate the globe. It may sound exciting, but I guarantee you, it was not.

All of a sudden, other countries in Southeast Asia were subject to severe contagion, including Malaysia and Indonesia.

Hong Kong

Hong Kong faced an ironic challenge. The territory had only just returned to Chinese control in July 1997. Prior to the transfer, most investors believed that Hong Kong was a safer investment than mainland China. Because Thailand's crisis was related to its fixed exchange rate, and since Hong Kong had a currency board, which requires the equivalent of a fixed exchange rate, investors feared that the currency board might be abandoned. This caused major disruptions in HK's usually smooth functioning financial markets.
The free-market laissez-faire HK government then surprisingly intervened in a massive way, but this time, it wasn't simply intervening in the financial system, but rather, under the leadership of then Finance Secretary Joseph Tsang, the government went on a buying spree, purchasing about $12 billion worth of shares in the HK stock market. The HK government was not immediately out of the woods. The territory would suffer a severe recession. Nonetheless, and more importantly, the peg held.

The irony of the HK crisis was that many observers thought that the Chinese government should help Hong Kong by intervening. We had a situation where supposedly *strong* Hong Kong, might need assistance from *weak* China. This was never contemplated as a scenario during the pre-turnover period.

Malaysia

The crisis spread to Malaysia. The government first reacted by raising interest rates. When that caused a recession and didn't stop a decline in the ringgit FX rate, the Malaysian government adopted a different approach than other East Asian countries. The government adopted capital controls. It required anyone selling a Malaysian stock, after having owned it for less than one year, to keep the proceeds of such sales in a Malaysian ringgit asset for at least one year. Trading in Malaysian stocks outside the country was also banned. Despite a recession, these controls enabled Malaysia to avoid the worst effects of the East Asian crisis.

Malaysia was always an interesting place to visit. About 70 percent of the population is Malay and Muslim. A little less than 25 percent of the population is Chinese, with the remainder being of Indian origin. Malays, called Bumiputras, have a much higher birthrate than the two other groups, slowly increasing their proportion of the total population.

Malaysia follows a racist government policy. Malays make up the bulk of the Bumiputra population. Some other non-Malays of *indigenous* origin are also classified as Bumiputras. Bumiputras are largely Muslim. It is *affirmative action* in the extreme. There are Bumiputra quotas for all sorts of activities. Although there is a debate about turning the country into a meritocracy, I doubt that will happen anytime soon.

Malaysia was the first Muslim majority country I had visited where there many female officials. I assumed most were Muslim women because they wore a headscarf. This was a sign that Malaysia was more flexible in its interpretation of Islam.

Indonesia

One of the most affected countries of contagion was Indonesia. Moody's had rated Indonesia a number of years before the East Asian crisis. In fact, I was the lead for that initial rating. The only strange thing to occur during the initial meetings with the government, was that during a meeting with the Finance Minister, suddenly TV cameras were introduced into the room. We were being filmed. Fortunately, the TV cameras were eventually removed, and the meeting returned to normal. It was just another example of how crazy the atmosphere around sovereign ratings was becoming. Even an initial meeting with a government official was deemed worthy, by some, of being broadcast on the evening news.

One of the major risks in Indonesia, well before 1997, was that the small Chinese community wielded enormous power throughout the economy. Some estimates the ethnic Chinese own about 70 percent of the nation's wealth. This, in and of itself, would not pose a risk, except that the overwhelming Malay Muslim majority held strong anti-Sinic beliefs. In the 1960s, the government forced the ethnic Chinese to choose either Indonesian citizenship or Chines citizenship. Dual citizenship was not allowed. The problem was that people who chose Chinese nationality were recognized as Chinese by the PRC. In addition, this forced most to change their names to Malay names.

Our concern was that if the economy ever were stressed again, the majority might turn against their Chinese neighbors, which they eventually did.

On the economic side, Indonesia was one of the countries seriously affected by lower oil prices in the early 1990s, the unified Chinese exchange rate and problems facing Japanese banks and the overall weakness of the Japanese economy.

For years, a growing proportion of non-oil exports was related to the assembly of electronics and similar consumer goods. Japanese firms used the ethnic Chinese-owned assembly plants located throughout Southeast Asia. With the sudden depreciation of the renminbi in 1994, Southeast Asian firms became increasingly uncompetitive with China. Added to that, financial and economic problems in Japan reduced overall export demand.

Indonesia had used controlled depreciation of its currency. Once the Thai baht collapsed in July 1997, the Indonesian rupiah wasn't far behind. Speculative attacks forced the government to allow the currency to float. As in Thailand, the FX rate plunged. That forced interest rates to rise exponentially, forcing most Indonesian firms into technical insolvency. As the domestic economy deteriorated rapidly, many ethnic Chinese left the country, causing a significant drain of human capital. This only made matters worse.

The decline in GDP was depression-like. The IMF put in place a major stabilization program. The political problem caused by the IMF program was not simply economic, but it was the optics that caused outrage.

The program was considered so important that the head of the IMF, the haughty Michel Camdessus went to Jakarta to witness the signing. Suharto, sitting at a table, with TV cameras rolling, was shown signing the agreement. Camdessus stood behind him with arms crossed. To most people who saw the image, it looked as though Camdessus was a harsh teacher chastising his student. To most Indonesians, this indicated that Suharto was no longer in control. The IMF was calling the shots. About four months after signing the agreement, Suharto was forced to resign after having been the leader of the country for 32 years. To this day, that image haunts the IMF. Bungling at its worst.

As expected, as the economic crisis grew worse, anti-Chinese sentiment rose to a fever pitch. In May 1998, there were full-blown riots aimed at the Chinese and their establishments. This triggered many Chinese-Indonesians to leave the country. Most did not return for years, making economic recovery even more difficult. The Chinese-Indonesians, who had been so important in helping to integrate Indonesia into the Southeast Asian Chinese trade cycle, were severely reduced in number, making it harder for the country to increase exports even though the rupiah had fallen to record lows against most major currencies. I have to say that racism remains a problem. Even recently there have been anti-Chinese increased anti-Chinese sentiment, but this time, having more to do with Indonesian Muslims moving towards a stricter interpretation of Islam than was previously the tradition. For instance, in 2017, the Christian Chinese-Indonesian governor of Jakarta was convicted of *blasphemy*, something that would not have been in the 1990s and sentenced to two years in prison.

One explanation for increased conservatism is that Islam, as a percentage of the population, is declining slowly but steadily. It is still by far the largest religious group in the country. The reason for the decline is not what we usually hear. The Christian population is rising by twice the rate of Muslim Indonesians. It gets more complex when regional differences are considered. All in all, Indonesia, the country with the largest Muslim population, is the only major Muslim-majority nation where the percentage of the Muslim population is declining will decline for the foreseeable future.

Indonesia and the Paris Club

As noted earlier, no one was sure what would happen if there was a default by a government on its international bonds subject to UK or New York law. Some were predicting if a country defaulted on international bonds, its entire financial system would seize up. External trade flows would cease because orders of attachment would be issued against sovereign assets. The IFIs wanted to see a country default on its bonds as a test case. The preference was for a *small* country, small in terms of international finance, not in size. Indonesia was to be the first test case.

To understand how this might be done, we have to know about rules surrounding Paris Club reschedulings. The Paris Club is an informal group of creditor country governments, dealing with bilateral or government-to-government debt.

One general requirement for rescheduling was that if creditor governments rescheduled debt, the commercial lenders to that country would also have to reschedule debt owed to them, along terms similar to terms given by the Paris Club.

The Paris Club is a strange *institution*. The meetings take place in Paris under the guidance of the French government. It's a well-known ploy by the French to make sure that negotiations with the borrowing country go well into the night, and even continuing non-stop until the next morning. Since there are several creditor governments, but on one borrower government, the pressure of the group is all on the borrowing country. The idea is to exhaust the negotiators of the borrowing country. This usually results in a deal more favorable to the creditor countries.

During the first big defaults starting with Mexico in 1982, the Paris Club changed one rule. It exempted international bonds from the conformity clause. International bonds were exempted from rescheduling along terms similar to the Paris Club. There were two reasons for this exception: 1) No one knew the consequences; and, 2) The amount of international bonds was small, so it wasn't worth the risk.

Most observers in the 1980 and 1990s didn't realize this had been an accommodation by the Paris Club. In the latter 1990s, the rules reverted to the original principle; conformity would include bonds.

In 1998, Indonesia needed a Paris Club rescheduling. The country had outstanding international bonds. It seemed the perfect *testcase*. However, Indonesia escaped being the first country to have its international bonds rescheduled in the modern era because conformity meant just that. The Paris Club had rescheduled principal, not interest. It turned out that Indonesian bonds didn't have any principal due for the time period dealt with by the Paris Club. Therefore, its bonds, for the moment, couldn't be forced into a rescheduling. The country dodged a bullet, but that didn't change its overall economic crisis. The IFIs would have to find another candidate for their experiment.

Korea

The pathway for the Korean crisis began in the early 1990s. Korea moved into current account deficit. There are numerous explanations. The world was in recession, the won had been appreciating and although the government restricted long-term foreign borrowing by business, short-term borrowing had no real restrictions, the most likely explanation being that the government viewed short-term borrowing as trade-related and not worrisome.

In order to finance growing current account deficits, foreign currency debt rose significantly. The country was starting to liberalize its banking system, with more banks being able to deal in foreign currency. Financial market liberalization peaking as Korea prepared to enter the OECD in 1996.

The country was sitting on a time bomb. By the end of 1996, over 60 percent of Korean bank liabilities were in foreign currency. There was a severe mismatch of currencies and maturities.

Nina Ramondelli, the backup analyst for Korea, with long experience in country risk analysis. argued that a crisis was brewing. She harped on problems developing in the banking system mismatches discussed above. It took a while for a committee to be convinced, but in the summer of 1997 a rating committee decided something unusual.

The Korean rating was to be downgraded by two notches from A1 to A3, without a rating review. Then for the second time in my time tenure at Moody's, senior management intervened. Instead of a double-notch downgrade, we were required to put the rating on review for downgrade. Senior management regarded a downgrade without a review would be too destabilizing.

Most of us were appalled by that. We never worried about the consequences of our actions. If we had, then investors would never know if we were telling them what we believed or what issuers and more importantly regulators might want them to believe.

We knew the government would use everything in its power to delay the final rating outcome. With no indication that we believed a two-notch rating downgrade was warranted. Instead of a sending a strong signal to investors, the signal was weakened to insignificance. In retrospect, as was the case with Thailand, those two management interventions into the rating process proved terribly wrong.

As expected, the rating review dragged on for months culminating in the two-notch downgrade. Yet, we knew the rating was under increasing pressure because the overall financial system was suffering not just from Korean-source risks, but from contagion that was sweeping across East Asia. The rating then fell another two-notches in December to Baa2. What changed everything were rumors that Korea's international reserves were not what they seemed. With our experience in Thailand, and problems caused by the government's manipulation of its international reserves, our analysts asked everything they could thing of about the country's international reserves.

In the end, it turned out that international reserves were almost non-existent because the government had deposited most of its foreign currency assets with Korean banks abroad. This proved disastrous.

As with Thailand, Korea's actions, if they had been undertaken by an advanced economy such as the UK, Germany or even Italy, there wouldn't have been a crisis. It is perfectly acceptable to include foreign currency deposits in private-sector commercial banks. Those deposits are highly liquid. Therefore, on the surface, when the government included deposits in Korean banks abroad in its international reserves, they were technically part of the country's reserves. The problem was that if the government withdrew the funds from those Korean banks, those banks would become insolvent. The implication was obvious; the government couldn't withdraw the funds and therefore, for all extents and purposes, it almost no foreign exchange.

This caused the rating to fall to Ba1 in early January 1998. That rating level, in retrospect, made the near-term crisis worse. This came to light only many months later. As I have said before, a rating agency can't consider the effects of a rating change. If it did, then markets would never know the rating agency's real opinion.

It turned out that because Korean bonds were the largest single source of Yankee bonds. Yankee bonds are bonds issued by a foreign issuer, denominated in dollars and sold in the US market. One of the largest single issuers was the Korean Development Bank (KDB). When Korea had an investment grade rating along with KDB, KDB bonds were included in investment grade Yankee bond indices. Once Korea's rating and thereby, KDB's rating, went below investment grade (Baa3), KDB bonds had to be removed from the index.

This caused a sudden, massive sell-off of KDB bonds, far beyond the credit risk associated with a Ba1 rating. The spread, or the interest differential between a riskless asset, such as US treasury securities, and market-determined interest rates went as high as 1,000 basis points. That kind of spread is usually associated with a high near-term default risk. We were quite confused by the market reaction. If anything, it made us worry even more about Korea risk. In the case of Korea, a stabilization program was quickly put in place, and the overall situation stabilized.

The US put pressure on the IMF and other G-7 countries to front-load any disbursements. Also, the US pressured creditor governments to put pressure on their commercial banks to rollover short-term debt, with an aim to rescheduling that debt in the near future. When I stay stabilized, I mean in terms of the rating, because the domestic economy was in turmoil, and would remain under stress for several years.

Following the crisis, on average, Korean GDP growth is lower than it had been in the pre-crisis period when it had been growing at so-called *Tiger* rates. In recent years growth has often been in the 2-3 percent range. Crises, especially caused by poor government policies, have consequences. Disinformation regarding economic statistics is never worth it. If exposed, the effects are severe and far-reaching.

Japan's Lost Decades

I have already discussed how the Japanese economy negatively affected East Asian economies prior to 1997. Between 1992 and 1994, Japanese GDP annual growth was less than 1.0 percent; anemic is putting it mildly. Growth picked up slightly in 1995 and 1996, but fell back to about 1.0 percent in 1997, with GDP actually declining in both 1998 and 1999. Making matters worse for East Asian countries involved the retreat of Japanese banks from foreign lending. Until the 1990s, Japanese banks had been significant sources of capital for East Asian firms.

Today, the 1990s in Japan is known as the *Lost Decade*. At Moody's we were living through the results. How did it happen? It all began with the 1985 Plaza Accord. When the Plaza Accord was signed, the Japanese yen exchange rate was Y242=US$1. By 1988, the yen had appreciated to Y120=$1 or by about 50 percent. This caused a massive credit bubble to develop throughout the Japanese economy, both in the stock market and in real estate.

The Nikkei stock market index peaked in December 1989 at 38,916. Some people were predicting that it would soon rise to 45,000. *Irrational Exuberance* at its most extreme. Price earnings ratios for Japanese corporations was quadruple that of US firms. Japanese growth depended on exports and investment in the export sector. With such a dramatic rise in the exchange rate, Japanese companies were under enormous competitive pressure.

The real estate bubble was actually worse than the stock market bubble. Prices in the late 1980s rose to unrealistic levels. For example, at one point the land on which the Imperial Palace in Tokyo stands was, on a square foot basis, worth more than all the real estate in California. The first signs of a deflating asset price bubble appeared in the real estate market. By 1988 and early 1989, instead of relentlessly rising, land prices began to stabilize. The stock market peaked in 1989. In 1989, monetary conditions began to tighten. In addition, a 3 percent consumption tax was imposed. Both policies contributed to a rapid negative change in economic sentiment.

Stock prices began to fall, and they kept falling. By the end of 1990, the Nikkei had plunged over 40 percent. This created a tremendous negative wealth effect. Land prices fell quickly. Within a brief time period, Japanese banks asset quality deteriorated across the board. This is what led to their withdrawal of credit in East Asia. Bank balance sheets were in terrible shape.

The government attempted to stimulate the economy through fiscal stimulus. The problem facing the Japanese government was that the size of the government sector was and still is relatively small compared to most advanced economies. Given that tax increases were off the table, spending had to increase. Once deficits grew, the government's debt-to-revenue ratio deteriorated. This is a much more important ratio than debt-to-GDP. Debt-to-revenue gives us an idea of how much revenue would need to rise, to reduce the debt burden relative to government income.

Throughout the 1990s, we saw deterioration across East Asia. At the time, the Japanese rating remained Aaa. By 1998, Japan's debt trajectory started to become problematic. With investor confidence in the region weakened we began to worry about Japanese government funding risk. The difference in the default risk between a Aaa and Aa1 is small, as noted above in the section on Canada. A Aaa implies that the investor doesn't have to consider any risk affecting repayment except for black swan events. With the growing debt, we finally downgraded Japan's rating to Aa1 in November 1998. This proved just the first of a number of rating downgrades.

The story was always the same. Slow growth led to slow revenue growth. Fiscal stimulus was applied, each time failing to produce the desired result. The banking system needed a massive bailout. The deterioration continued throughout the 1990s. In fact, for all intents and purposes, the deterioration continued through the first decade of 21st century. Some say Japan experienced not just a lost decade, but a lost 20 years (and more).

This is not intended to be a primer on sovereign risk analysis. That would require a separate book altogether. What I do know is that changing Japan's sovereign ratings had enormous implications.

The rating fell to Aa2 in September 2000, falling once again in December 2001 to Aa3. It then further declined to A2 in May 2002.

Not only did these downgrades shock the Japanese government, but they created a journalistic firestorm that was even worse than what happened with the Canadian and Italian ratings.

On many occasions, I went to Japan to give briefings on the economy, usually to packed auditoriums. I met regularly with journalists. The Japanese are as infatuated with *Dietrologia* as the Italians. I don't read Japanese, but I have been told that there were numerous books written in Japanese about the anti-Japan *conspiracy* I was so supposed to be involved in.

A brief word about conspiracy theories. As you know by now, I have been accused of being at the center of many conspiracies. Negative rating changes always required some nefarious forces of evil working against the country in question. Often, we were accused of timing rating outlook or rating reviews to coincide with political events in the country. Others assumed that we were an arm of the US government, being a kind of US *Enforcer*.

Nothing could have been further from the truth. Timing of rating events had to be adjusted, not to political events, but to rating committee scheduling issues. We needed to make sure all the appropriate people would be able to attend. This was not always easy. Scheduling became constrained by time zone differences between New York and the countries where analysts were located. Analyst vacations to places where there was no phone service sometimes created a problem. We actually had analysts who liked to mountain climb, and trek through the wilderness. Occasionally, analysts were too sick to take part in a long teleconference. Holidays posed another problem. The bottom line is that despite all the accusations I ever heard about the timing of a rating action, the reality was that humdrum issues determined timing. Timing had nothing to do with stealth.

My other take on conspiracies is that they would require a lot of coordination. We were barely able to get committees organized on a specific day, never mind being able to secretly coordinate the direction a rating would need to move in order to fulfill part of some grandiose plan. I know that neither I, nor the other analysts who worked alongside me, had such extraordinary organizational abilities. We were sovereign analysts, not CIA or NSA operatives. Turning me and others into CIA operatives might make for an interesting movie plot. It's just not based on reality. However, if there are any Hollywood types out there who would like to do just that, I would be glad to help.

It got so crazy, at one point, whenever I went to Japan, a press release would be issued by the Tokyo office to indicate the nature of my trip. Otherwise, the Japanese press was interpreting every trip as setting the stage for another downgrade.

On one trip to Tokyo, a reporter asked me if I was there for a rating announcement during my visit. I explained to him that it would be highly unlikely that I would be in the country when undertaking a rating action. I told him I would need to be in the home office, because a rating action entailed lots of logistical details, more easily accomplished at my office in New York. His response brought a smile to my face. He said, "Then when are you leaving?"

The Japanese Diet required the lead analyst for Japan as well as the head of East Asia to testify before a special committee. That was the first-time foreigners had been brought in to testify before the Diet since the 1976 testimony given by US executives involved in the infamous Lockheed Scandal. That scandal marked a watershed in Japanese politics and business practices. The former Prime Minister Kakuei Tanaka was convicted accepting bribes from Lockheed. As an aside, despite his conviction, Mr. Tanaka has been resurrected by some in Japan as a political genius.

Given the gravity of the reason for the first testimony by foreigners before the Diet, it seemed to us excessive. In Japanese eyes, our actions were viewed as far more sinister. Fortunately, Tom Byrne, then the lead analyst was well versed in East Asian protocol. He made sure he bowed appropriately before the committee. In the end, after the testimony, neither the Diet nor the government did anything harmful to Moody's.

One unexpected consequence of the Japanese downgrades was that in 2003, John Rutherfurd, Moody's new CEO, wanted to better understand sovereign ratings. He considered it a black box, which he didn't like. He wanted us to explain our ratings using more mathematics.

To date, no one, including the IFIs have been able to produce an accurate sovereign default model. Statistical problems include the small sample size, the difficulty in defining a sovereign default, and collinearity (where one change affects another). Anyway, when the CEO asked, we tried, but we couldn't predict sovereign defaults using a mathematical model. We found we could predict our own ratings using economic statistics and one index. It all boiled down to four variables for the foreign currency rating and four variables for the domestic currency rating. The model worked well, with an R-squared in the mid-80s. Outliers were few and easy to explain. This first model was only updated after my tenure at Moody's.

The four variables for the foreign currency rating predictor model consisted of GDP per capita, GDP growth, foreign debt/exports ratio and the World Bank Governance Index. The only difference between this model and the local currency government bond rating was instead of the foreign debt/exports ratio, the government debt/revenue ratio was used.

I always found it amusing seeing models used to predict particular sovereign ratings, or better yet, to explain sovereign ratings ex post. I would read academic articles *explaining* Moody's sovereign ratings. It was truly weird to see attempts to model our thought processes. Since I had sat on the committees determining such ratings, I knew exactly what was said and debated. Except for really controversial ratings, sovereign rating committees rarely had more than ten voting members. As the years passed, the number kept inching higher, but it was rarely large.

Most important for us, we satisfied John Rutherfurd. It's always good to keep the boss happy.

Another aside about Mr. Rutherfurd; he was known to have a terrible temper. I never witnessed it, but I was told by many others who experienced it first-hand. When angry, I was told he would shout and once reportedly threw a computer against a wall. The laptop was not working right. In all fairness, how many of us would have loved, at certain times, to have been able to toss an uncooperative computer? I repeat, I never witnessed this side of him. Others, too, noticed that John didn't yell at me.

Whenever dinners included John, either with a large group of Moody's managing directors or for smaller staff gatherings, I was always seated next to him. I was told the reason was that he seemed to treat me well. He had bright white hair, wore glasses, and usually had a smile on his face whenever I saw him. He was another example of that now rarely heard, upper-class Northeast accent, similar to the nurse at DeWitt. To be honest, we always had great conversations on various topics, from history to art. He had traveled extensively throughout Asia and had a particular admiration for, and knowledge of, India. Although this was considered an *assignment* by others, it was always a pleasure for me. After a few minutes, we were always laughing at something.

I should say that John was not the only one who was known for having a temper. The other man was Tom McGuire. He is brilliant. As I noted earlier, he was probably the single person most responsible for creating the modern credit rating agency business model. He understood ratings better than anyone I have ever met.

He was a big man, with a deep voice and oozed *gravitas*. Perhaps his Jesuit educational background could explain his penchant for putting medieval torture tools on the table during rating committees. Thank goodness he never used them, but it made for great theater. He didn't really shout at analysts at rating committees even if he thought they were being illogical in their argument or lacking sufficient knowledge in the area under discussion. However, he had a razor-sharp tongue that could devastate an analyst in his line of sight.

In the early 1990s, the sovereign team was small. Therefore, most of us sat on almost every sovereign rating committee. We observed each other's behavior. One of the amusing things to watch was when Tom would get angry with Guillermo Estebanez. Guillermo was an analyst who came from Spain and still retained a strong Spanish accent. He was polar opposite to Tom in appearance. Instead of big, slightly menacing and deliberative in his speech, Guillermo was short, skinny and spoke at a breathtaking pace, Spanish accent and all.

Whenever, Tom would try to stop Guillermo, using Tom's usual intimidation technique, no matter the effort, Guillermo seemed oblivious. He just went on and on, making his point at lightning speed. Of course, this always made Tom angrier. Other committee members would just smile to ourselves and simply enjoyed the show.

As noted earlier, Tom was adept at creating an aura around ratings when ratings were little known outside of municipal finance. Part of his strategy was to keep us a bit mysterious. By the late 1990s, senior management began to ask outside consultants to survey how the investment community and issuers viewed Moody's compared to S&P.

The result was eye-opening. The surveys showed most issuers disliked or even hated Moody's. Most investors liked Moody's. S&P was liked by both issuers and investors. This worried management. Most revenues were derived from issuers. If they didn't like us, then if any alternative appeared they might move their business. The response was to give every analyst and managing director lessons on *how to be nice*. I'm not making this up; we had to sit through hours of training programs to be trained in how to be civil to others.

Many analysts had a problem with that friendlier approach. They were perfectly satisfied with our traditional standoffishness. From that time on, we were all ordered to treat issuers better, with specific rules on how to do that. It seemed reasonable to me that we should be friendlier with our main revenue source. However, detailed instructions on precisely how to do that was a bit absurd.

Starting with these training sessions on *niceness*, Moody's slowly became an outwardly friendlier place. Fashions come and go, as Professor Kirkpatrick pointed out, nothing stays the same.

Fortunately, I was not there for the most recent changes, which followed the financial crisis. Today, everything is regulated and bureaucratized. Regulators think ratings must be perfect, forgetting that they are based on opinion, not scientific certitude. I have been told by many that the work environment at rating agencies is unpleasant compared to the glory days of the 1990s.

Rating the USA

Another interesting rating action took place in January 1996. We put the rating of $387 billion of US Federal government debt on review for possible downgrade. I was the lead analyst. This was a truly unusual review because default risk wasn't related to the ability to pay, but to willingness. We were in the middle of the nation's first debt ceiling crisis. It seems little has changed since then. We weren't sure if the government might actually miss a payment on a maturing Treasury security or interest coming due on bonds.

What made this review extra-special was that included in the press release, we indicated that even if the rating was downgraded, and even if there was a default on some Treasury securities, the rating on those securities would not go lower than Aa1. This was an unprecedented action, putting a floor on the rating even if in default.

The reason this was the right thing to do related to Moody's definition of a rating. Moody's weren't technically pure default risk ratings. They had embedded in them the expected loss resulting from default. S&P ratings were pure default ratings. If the US government missed a principal or interest payment, S&P's rating would have to D for default. We argued that even if the US government defaulted on either principal or interest, the default would be remedied immediately. That meant that sending a signal of a much lower rating was inappropriate. Telling investors that in the event of a default, it would be so short-term that the loss incurred would be *de minimus*. If the default were to occur, then some signal was needed to indicate that small risk, in an otherwise *risk-free* secure security. Limiting the outcome to Aa1 did just that. In the end, the rating was confirmed at Aaa as the debt ceiling was raised in time.

There was another fascinating twist to this story. We had identified the total of $387 billion of securities that were on review. There was no way for investors to determine which particular securities in their own portfolios would be subject to the review because CUSIP numbers were aggregated for these instruments. No one before the 1996 review for downgrade had ever thought that necessary. As a consequence, starting in October 1996, Treasury bonds were given more fully informed CUSIP numbers.

When most countries are put on review for downgrade, the government protested, sometimes, vehemently as witnessed in my descriptions above regarding Italy, Canada and Japan. In the case of the US, the reaction was totally different.

The US Treasury was helpful and appeared fully supportive of the review. Why? The source of the debt ceiling problem was Congressional intransience. It was controlled by the GOP. Clinton was the President. Our review had absolutely nothing to do with any recommendations from government officials. However, a review played into the hands of the President, helping him to push Congress to quickly raise the debt ceiling. It represented another unintended consequence of delaying the rise in the debt ceiling.

I believed then, and I do now, that a debt ceiling is one of the dumber things the Federal government does. There is absolutely no reason to have such a ceiling. It makes the US look like a laughing stock around the world. The debt ceiling requires that even if an expenditure is approved by Congress, the Treasury may not be allowed to fund it going forward. My issue is, how can a debt ceiling potentially prevent repayment of interest and principal for previously, legislatively, approved bonds? It's ridiculous.

As the US federal government debt became a more important issue in the 1990s, I spent an increasing amount of time exploring the nature of that debt, especially when I became a managing director in 1996.

A big issue in Italy, Canada and Japan centered around national government pension systems. Dealing with pensions is a tricky business. Pension promises are not debt. In the corporate and sub-sovereign world, pensions are usually legally binding. Existing pensions usually can't be changed ex post. They only can be changed going forward. National governments are different. They can change all pension promises even already existing ones, and frequently do.

There is a strong argument to calculate long-term pension costs for national governments using FRSB (Financial Reporting Standards Board) generally accepted accounting principles. In the 1990s, such measures for measuring pensions were only used by the New Zealand and Australian governments. At the time, the best number frequently produced was based on Net-Present-Value (NPV), an adequate, but far from perfect measure of the pension burden.

This first became important for the Italian rating because if future pension costs were included in the total implied debt using NPV, the ratio equaled about 600 percent of GDP.

In 1995, Italy adopted the so-called *Dini Reform* of the pension system. There were important changes in made to pensions far out into the future, but little changed regarding near-term pension expenditures. However, when subject to NPV analysis, the implied Italian government debt, including pensions, went from about 600 percent of GDP down to less than 300 percent. It demonstrated to me how sensitive such estimates could be even to minor near-term changes in a pension system.

I studied national pensions a lot, given pension issues, not only in Italy, but also in Canada and Japan. Although the US debt ceiling controversy was not related to Social Security, the US alone among advanced countries that calculates the difference between what Social Security income is as part of the funding of the deficit. The US, uniquely, calculates Federal government debt including the accumulated Social Society funds, which helped finance past deficits. International comparisons of US Federal government debt, using the government's approach, overstates the debt when comparing it to other countries. Until countries start to use FRSB accounting across the board, including balance sheets based on FRSB rules, we can't really compare pensions across nations. I wound up writing an article for *The Washington Quarterly* on pensions. As a result, I was asked to testify before Congress.

I learned a lot about life fundamentals from that research. At the most basic level, I realized that we only exist in the present, the on-going present. Your reaction might be, so what? We all know that. What I learned from that was the incredible that this trite idea had huge implications for politics and economics.

Since there is never a future, and the past is already gone, discussions about future economic policy are philosophical illusions. We, and I include myself, are prone to say that we need this or that policy in order to affect the economy in the future. Those policies need to be implemented through the political process. It seems straightforward, but it isn't.

The reality is that all we ever have is income and wealth distribution in the present. We may have endless debates about what will happen five or ten years from now. What we really need to concentrate on is what's going on now.

That's all that counts. Pensions will be adjusted in the future if society decides that it wants to either spend more or spend less on pensions. Setting up national pension plans are not worth the paper the laws are printed on. Governments, at any time in future, can do whatever society wants them to do. The same is equally true for every aspect of our lives. We can create the illusion that we are in control of the future, but that is the worst illusion of all.

My views regarding pensions and other entitlements became more widely known. As a result, I was asked to join the *Global Commission on Aging*. I have joked, for years, that the only reason I was qualified to join that commission was that I'm aging.

I wound up participating in interesting meetings organized by the commission. They always were held in beautiful locations, which I would never have visited otherwise. One takeaway from being on the commission, was that pension problems, which will emerge in the sense that unless governments decide to kill huge numbers of us, there will be more old people across the planet, in every country. Since I will make a leap of faith that governments aren't going to suddenly euthanize the elderly *en masse*, in the future, society will have to deal with all of us. Discussing pensions is packed with heightened emotions on all sides, the young having one perspective and the elderly another. Despite the emotional nature of national pensions, it is not the biggest problem facing societies worldwide. Rationing medical care is a much bigger public policy issue. Let's forget about the future. We must decide how to supply healthcare to people now. The level of benefits differs from country to country, and the way healthcare is delivered, also differs. There is one fundamental that never changes. Healthcare has no upper limit on the amount of healthcare resources people will desire.

How many times we visit doctors, how quickly medical services are delivered, the manner in which those services are delivered together determine immediate costs. Society has to decide what qualifies people to be healthcare suppliers, in other words, who can be a doctor, nurse or other healthcare provider. Will getting a prescription require a doctor or physician's assistant approval, or will pharmacists be allowed to provide medications without a medical order? How much psychological treatments will society allow?

The most difficult issue, especially in the US, is not how many people will be covered by healthcare, but when does society say that a very sick person, with no likelihood of recovery, or of living for much longer, even with very expensive procedures, should they receive that expensive care? Who decides? The individual? The family? Society? In the end, the choice will be society's alone.

In the real world, this moral dilemma has real consequences. There is some misunderstanding regarding end-of-life expenses. Overall, the cost is not extraordinarily high relative to all healthcare spending.

The problem is that in the US, Medicare, the government program aimed towards the elderly, spends about 25 percent of its expenditures on the last 12 months of life. I never would have imagined country risk analysis would include discussions fundamental moral issues, normally outside economic discourse.

This next section involves one of the most important events, not just in my life, but in the life of the nation. That's 9/11.

Life in *Old New York*

For discussing the specifics of what happened that day, a little background on where I lived, prior to 9/11, may be useful.

Where I lived upon returning to New York is representative of developments in the life of the city. At first, I rented an apartment in the southern most section of Westchester County, near where my parents and other family members lived. My commute to Wall Street was long. I had to drive to the train station. Then, I boarded a commuter train to Grand Central Station. From there, I took the subway down to Wall Street.

In the late 1970s-early 1980s, New York City was still recovering from its 1975 financial crisis, which had resulted in the city defaulting of its bonds. The New York State had to come to the rescue and control most aspects of the city's finances. At the same time, New York State's budget was under pressure. The state cut expenditures. I remember when I returned to New York, the highest state marginal income tax rate was an incredible 12 percent. Only four years earlier, the rate was 15.35 percent. Over the decades that rate has been cut by more than half.

With strict austerity, maintenance was postponed. There was a major subway strike beginning on April 1. The *April Fools* strike lasted for 11 days. Mayor Koch stood his ground. The city refused to cave to the subway union. For 9 workdays, my commute was tortuous. Beginning on

April 1, when I arrived in Grand Central Station, I was forced to either walk from 42nd Street to Wall Street or walk to the Path trains to New Jersey. If I used the Path route, I could take a train to Hoboken and then take another train to the World Trade Center (WTC). Walking to the Path trains from Grand Central took about thirty minutes. On arriving at the WTC, there was another fifteen-minute walk to my office. I tried both ways. They were equally exhausting. Fortunately, the strike occurred in April, so extreme weather was avoided I kept asking myself, why did I leave Charlotte?

The subway strike was finally resolved, and things went back to normal, which wasn't that great to begin with. The commuter trains needed heavy duty maintenance. They often stalled, or the heating or air conditioning systems didn't work. In the end, air conditioning, or the lack thereof, proved the final straw.

In August 1980, twice within about two weeks, the air conditioning broke down. The problem was train cars were sealed. Windows didn't open. The trains were always crowded with no possibility of air circulation. It was stifling and unbearable, far worse than traveling on the subways in the pre-airconditioned era. Subways had fans, and the windows could be opened.

Besides air conditioning, trains were not receiving the general maintenance required. The result: my trains were delayed twice within about two weeks. It took two-and-a-half hours to go from Grand Central to Westchester compared to a normal time of about 30 minutes. After two back-to-back trains with no air conditioning in a hot New York summer, I reached my limit. My lease was up in September. I moved to Manhattan.

The New York City subway system in Manhattan has several routes on the West Side. In 1980, there was only one subway route going down the East Side. In the pre-WW II, that made sense, but as Manhattan neighborhoods changed over time, one subway line serving the East Side no longer made sense. The Lexington Avenue line was constantly over-crowded. With so many lines on the West Side, they would get crowded, but not as badly as the Lexington Avenue line.

Crowding was not the determining factor, but rather my memory of the subway strike. I wanted to be able to walk to work, if necessary and/or I wanted to be able to take the PATH trains to reach downtown.

West Side neighborhoods were far more complex than the East Side. Safe areas were located in a patchwork of small neighborhoods. This was a time when the City still had a high crime rate.

In the end, I chose an apartment on W. 23rd Street, between 6th and 7th Avenues. Both avenues had subway lines, with a PATH station on 6th Avenue. It was in the heart of Chelsea. Today, Chelsea is an incredibly chic neighborhood. When I lived there, it was getting better, but there were still SROs (single room occupancy), which usually housed very low-income people and/or people with mental issues. It was only in the very first stage of gays moving north from Greenwich Village because of rapidly rising rents.

I found a great studio apartment in a newly renovated doorman loft building. It had 12-foot ceilings, allowing for a small, crawl space loft bedroom. I lived there for two years. I decided it was time to buy an apartment. I was being paid a fairly high salary for someone my age, but then as now, Manhattan condos or coops were expensive.

I explored neighborhoods in Brooklyn, New Jersey and marginal neighborhoods in Manhattan. My parents always accompanied me in my search. I found an apartment on West 42nd Street. It was a newly renovated loft building, which had been an armory. Later, I found out that a cousin's husband had actually served there when he was younger.

When I showed it to my parents, my mother said she liked it better than Hoboken. That decided it. I bought it.

The neighborhood was edgy, and that's putting it mildly. W. 42nd Street was notorious. It was filled with every criminal activity you could imagine. Since I didn't have children, it didn't pose a problem. Also, there were many subway lines accessible near Times Square.

Given the notoriety of W. 42nd Street, when people would ask me where I lived, knowing that I worked at One Wall

Street, my West 42nd Street response always resulted in dead silence. They had no idea what to say. It was certainly not what they had expected. I have to admit, I loved when that happened.

I lived there for many years. I only decided to move out when my son was born. Although the neighborhood had improved over the years, it was not a good neighborhood for small children. Recently, I have visited the *old neighborhood,* but today, the West 42nd Street, between 10th Avenue and West Street (12th Avenue), is filled with high rise luxury apartment buildings, some of which are over sixty stories high.

Living on West 42nd Street was an eyeopener for me. Although the main entrance was on 42nd Street, my condo looked out onto West 43rd Street. Our building was the only fully occupied apartment building. There was a small apartment building that was being occupied by squatters and people who were still fighting eviction because the landlord wanted to tear it down.

The place is near to the entrance to the Lincoln Tunnel. Most people driving by had no idea that people were now living on West 43rd Street. This was at the beginning of the AIDS epidemic. I was shocked to see that many commuters would stop their cars under my windows and have sex with a prostitute of questionable sexuality out in the open. My first thoughts were how could these guys usually in suits have sex in the street with a hooker and then they would be returning to the families in New Jersey. It was unbelievable.

One of the first big changes in neighborhood safety was when a forty-story building was built on my block. Now, everyone knew that people lived on West 42nd-43rd Streets. More importantly, that building had balconies. When hookers would show up on the street near the building, some people would throw water from their balcony onto the hooker and the john. With so many balconies, there was no way anyone could see where the water had come from. That reduced prostitution dramatically.

The Armory was filled with many people in the arts. We had a famous bandleader and the Director of the New York City Opera. Next door to him was a guy who tuned pianos in Lincoln Center. There were famous singers, photographers, musicians, actors, textile designers; the list could go on and on.

One night, when walking back to the apartment with a gay friend who appeared in daytime soap operas, we passed a hooker at the corner of 42nd Street and 10th Avenue, the hooker propositioned us. My friend's response is classic. He said in a slight southern accent, "I'm not interested, unless you can strap it on!" That shut up the hooker. We simply laughed and went on our way.

9/11

About 6 months after my son's birth, we decided to move to New Jersey. We lived in a comfortable suburb, with a short commute for the suburbs, but longer than when living in Manhattan. After a few years, we grew to miss the City. I decided we should rent an apartment and see if we were comfortable living in a city apartment with a young and active boy. At the same time, we needed to find a safe neighborhood with a good public elementary school. The answer was to move to Battery Park City, which was about 15-minute walk to work, very safe for children, with a local public school that was rated among the better ones in the City. We moved there in May 2001.

We kept the New Jersey home, just in case we found living in Manhattan with children a little too challenging. We found a beautiful apartment, with great views of the harbor, the World Trade Center and the World Financial Center, just across the street from the WTC.

It was really a great place to live. My son was enrolled in kindergarten at P.S. 89, just a short walk away. His first day of school was on September 10. Parents were able to stay with the kindergarten students for the first day. The next day, parents could stay, but only in the hallways.

Of course, I walked with my son, and we stayed there on Monday. On Tuesday, since I couldn't stay in the classroom, I left my son with his other parent. This proved quite lucky for me. Normally, I walked to work via the foot bridge across West Street going to the World Trade Center, either by walking along the north walkways of the WTC, or in inclement weather, through the WTC mall, where I had walked in 1993, during the first bombing. I should add that unless there was an important meeting, I usually arrived at work sometime after 9 AM. On September 11, I walked to work from several blocks north of the WTC. Also, because my son's school started a bit earlier than 9, I wound up arriving at the office slightly before 9 AM.

At the same time, a cousin, who needed special eye surgery at Manhattan Eye and Ear Hospital, was staying with us. She lived in the far northern suburbs. From our apartment, she could take a short taxi ride to the hospital. As many know, you often have to go to a hospital very early in the morning when having surgery. In her case, she left the apartment around 6 AM. She left most of her belongings at the apartment thinking she could get them when she was released.

After I arrived at my office, I was sitting in my office, which didn´t have a direct view of the WTC. All of sudden, the building shook. The windows rattled. I immediately got up and went to David Levey´s office, which had a direct view of the World Trade Center. We both looked out the windows and could see a massive hole in the North Tower. It was huge and oval in shape. We looked at each other in astonishment. From the hole in the building and the noise we heard prior to the crash, it was obvious to us that a plane had struck the building. We debated how could a plane crash into the building on such a bright and clear day. We talked about different this was compared to the plane that crashed into the Empire State Building in the 1930s.

Since both David and I had lived through enough international political intrigue, we immediately thought it was terrorism. An announcement came over the PA system telling us at first to remain where we were. Then soon after, another announcement told us to go to the basement and stay there. It was soon announced that the second tower had been hit. There was no doubt this was terrorism, not a freak accident.

When I heard that, I remembered a recent terrorist attack in in the Middle East, where a bomb caused a building to collapse like a pancake, killing everyone inside. I thought there is no way I would remain there and certainly I was not going to the basement.

I walked outside on Church Street, just about one block north of the WTC. The police were telling us we had to go towards the East River. I went to a policewoman and said I needed to go towards West Street because my son was in school there. She said OK. The air was still clear. In just a few minutes, I reached the school. We left to go to the apartment.

On arriving, from our 22nd floor apartment, all I could see was the World Financial Center. Behind it, only smoke was visible. At first, we decided to go the ferries, which were a

2'minute walk from the apartment and go directly to New Jersey.

Then all of a sudden, the dark gray smoke which had been behind the World Financial Center, suddenly began to cross the walkway, inundating the ferry terminal in a dense dark cloud that was many stories high. Obviously, getting to the ferry was out of the question. It was time to leave the apartment. My ex took my son and our two small dogs down the stairs. Taking an elevator would have been too dangerous. I then got all the most essential documents I thought we might need. I carefully closed every window, and pulled down the blinds, as though pulling down the blinds would make a difference.

When I got to the lobby, my family was not there because the police ordered everyone to leave as soon as they reached the ground floor. I went outside and then walked towards West Street. By then, there were massive numbers of people walking north, in total silence. I needed to find my family. It took a few minutes, but we were able to meet just a short distance north on West Street. My son was sitting in his stroller, and the two dogs, our Shetland sheep dog and Lhasa Apso walking alongside.

We decided that we should walk to our church, the Church of the Ascension on 5th Avenue between 10th and 11th. We knew it would take about 40 minut3s to walk there.

As we were approaching Chambers Street, we heard a terrible noise. Everyone turned around. Then we watched as the second tower collapsed in front of our eyes. I can't describe the feeling of seeing that, knowing that not everyone would have escaped.

We were particularly lucky, because we had left soon enough that we were not covered in any smoke or dust. Many others were not so lucky.

We arrived at our church. Everything looked perfect. There was no dust or smoke there. You could see that the two towers, which were once visible from 5th Avenue, were gone, replaced by a tower of dark gray smoke. Everyone at church was totally devastated. It was all too hard to comprehend. Cell phones weren't working. Later, I heard that texting was still working. This was at a time when texting was not yet as popular as it is now. I never even thought of trying to text.

I needed to contact my cousin. I used landline phones in the church. I couldn't get through to the hospital to let my cousin know that we were safe. After several different attempts to contact people, I finally reached my cousin's mother who lived in the northern suburbs. I told her that when she hears from her daughter, please let her know we are OK.

I needn't go into how we our spent time, because everyone was simply on edge. After several hours, we heard that Penn Station on 34th Street was open. From there we could take a train to our Maplewood home. The subways were still running but were skipping stops near the World Trade Center. We decide we were going to give it a try. With my son in a stroller and with two dogs, we walked to the nearest train, which could get us to Penn Station. The subway ride was free. I don't know if that was an official policy, or just determined by the local station supervisor.

The dogs were with us and had their one and only subway ride. Only service dogs were allowed on the subway. This was not a usual time.

I will never forget our arrival at Penn Station. The station is regularly crowded and filled with noise. Today, it was wall-to-wall people, with no one saying anything. The silence was deafening. Everyone was lined up in orderly lines. As trains arrived, they were quickly filled to capacity, and sent out to New Jersey. No one, including the police, said a word about our two dogs going on the train. It took quite a long time before we were able to board a train. This train was going to Penn Station, Newark. At that time, trains to Maplewood only departed from Broad Street Station, another major rail hub in Newark.

When we arrived at Penn Station, we were met by people with bus schedules asking where we needed to go. I said Broad Street Station. We were then told where to go to get a bus that would take us there. We got on the bus and in a few minutes arrived at Broad Street. I saw a policeman and asked if there would be a problem bring the dogs onboard. He said, if anyone gives you a problem, just let me know.

Sure enough, when we were getting on the train, the conductor said we couldn't because we had two dogs. I told him what the policeman had just said. He reluctantly acquiesced. I thought that conductor was an idiot, and that's putting it mildly.

In a short time, we arrived at the Maplewood station. We were quite surprised to find there were jitneys parked there able to take us to our home. It was amazing. The trip from church to home took about four-and-a-half hours. However, everything was incredibly well organized. I was pleasantly shocked.

It was great being *home*. We didn't need anything because the house was still fully furnished, including clothes. We were without our car. I parked it under the American Express Building in the World Financial Center. I had no idea if the car had survived the disaster.

Our next-door neighbors lent us one of their cars. The next day, I went and bought a new car. The salesmen were surprised to see anyone that day buying a new car. I thought to myself, at least I'm helping the economy a little in this time of crisis.

As a family, we would not move back to the city until the following February. The problem was that the fires at the site were burning well into January. The air was too polluted for my son, and my baby daughter, who was born six days later on September 17.

Moody's headquarters was closed. I heard it was shrouded in dust. The building, remarkably, wasn't damaged by the attack. Some people from Moody's volunteered to return to the building under police supervision to try to get laptops from offices, so that work could continue. I can't imagine how difficult and dangerous that was, given the fumes, asbestos and other pollutants in the air.

Shortly, the staff was contacted, indicating where they could pick up their laptops. Those who lived in Manhattan who were not directly were asked to go to offices, which I was told had been lent to us by some investment banks. I was sent to a hotel in nearby Short Hills to pick up my laptop. From that day onwards, we functioned as though nothing had happened. Planning certainly paid off. In addition, technology made it doable, something that wouldn't have been possible just a decade before. Having a large London, Paris, Frankfurt and Tokyo offices, fully integrated together produced a seamless transition to the new reality.

For family reasons, we had to fly several weeks after 9/11. That was another eerie experience. The airports were desolate, with almost no one there. We had first class tickets, but we were the only people on the plane. The flight attendants gave my children royal treatment, especially my baby daughter. They were genuinely grateful we were flying. For them, our family represented a bit or normality, something sorely missed by everyone.

Despite the terrorist attack, I decided to stay in Battery Park City. Instead of continuing to rent an apartment, I thought it was time to buy. When I mentioned this to other people, they gave me strange looks, seeming to say, "Are you crazy?' Nonetheless, I went to a local realtor in January. We had been renting a two-bedroom apartment. With the addition of our daughter, a three-bedroom apartment was required.

The realtor showed me a three-bedroom apartment where the owners had left and decided they didn't want to return to the area. This was a common response. The apartment was in perfect condition. Every room and even one of the bathrooms looked out at the Upper Bay, the Statue of Liberty, Ellis Island, Staten Island and Jersey City. It was breathtaking.

The owners were in a hurry to sell, so I was able to buy the apartment at an incredibly low price. I would still need a small mortgage to finance it. That proved a challenge. The big banks all refused to even look at giving me a mortgage because there had been no sales of a three-bedroom apartment south of Canal Street since 9/11. There were no comps, or similar sales to use for apprising the apartment. Then the realtor called and suggested I try Valley National Bank, a small local bank, originally based in Long Island, but with plans to expand.

After some deliberation by their staff, Valley National came up with an ingenious solution. Instead of looking for comps based on the number of rooms, they would allow comps, in this case, to be made using price per square foot comparables. Since there had been a few sales of smaller apartments, we now had comps. The mortgage was approved. We were able to move in, in May 2002.

Several months after the purchase, I ran into the realtor on the street. He told me that after my apartment got a mortgage, that provided a comparable and then there was a stream of three-bedroom apartments sold.

I don't think people know important Valley National Bank was in helping people to return and/or stay in the area. The banking team deserves kudos for their foresight and courage. It reminded me of the famous story about Amadeo Giannini. He founded the Bank of Italy in America in 1904, later changed to Bank of America. His bank provided bank services to poor Italian immigrants, which the other banks didn't want to do because of anti-Italian immigrant discrimination.

When the great earthquake struck in 1906, instead of shutting his doors, Giannini was able to begin lending on a makeshift desk in the open air. His ability to get money from his bank vault and his courage to restart lending led to more than a century of success.

The Government was worried that people might not return to live in downtown, which had been expanding over the years. To provide an extra incentive to stay or move there, the Federal government gave $1000 per month for two years to all households who lived south of Canal Street, including resident owners and renters. It wouldn't have made a difference in our case, because we were going to stay, no matter what. It did have a big impact on keeping and attracting new renters. It also made some owners to stay put instead of leaving the area. It worked. Downtown was slowly able to recover, and is, once again, a thriving place to live and work.

The Euro

Despite all these disruptions, life went on. I was being kept busy with the collapse of the Argentine economy, discussed earlier. In addition, the euro had been becoming more important in assessing sovereign risk in member countries. It is worth looking into the history of the euro to understand many economic and political developments since then.

In 1989, the Berlin Wall fell. It was obvious that the two Germanies would soon be reunited. The President of France, Francois Mitterrand and the Chancellor of West Germany, Helmut Kohl met to discuss the implications of German unification. Both wanted to make sure that the new Germany stayed anchored to the West and not set its eyes on the East, something that had caused so much misery and death during the two world wars.

They came up with an ingenious idea; create an EU currency. Once a member, Germany would be securely anchored to the West. That concept became enshrined the Maastricht Treaty, which was signed in 1991. That treaty said the EU should aim to create an EU-wide currency. In all fairness, almost from the very start of the *European Project*, there had been a desire to create a European Monetary Union (EMU). It's just that many distractions kept pushing the start date further and further into the future.

With the renewed momentum created by the need to anchor a united Germany to the West, it was time to implement specific policies to lead to EMU. The first step was the creation of EMS (European Monetary System) followed by the ERM (Exchange Rate Mechanism). ERM introduced currency bands. Governments had to aim to keep their exchange rates within certain parameters, set in percentage terms, around a baseline. The baseline exchange rate was the ECU (European Currency Unit), an artificial unit of account based on the weighted average of member exchange rates.

The ERM quickly came under attack by speculators causing the UK to leave the ERM in September 1992. Italy suspended ERM membership until it rejoined in 1996. Britain had been in recession in the early 1990s. Trying to keep within the currency band set for it, prolonged the recession. Italy's problems were actually worse because the ERM caused the country to lose competitiveness vis-à-vis Germany and other ERM countries. As usual, Italian society as discussed above, had a hard time enacting fundamental economic reform. Having a currency band, even a very wide one, meant that some of the loss of competitiveness could be reduced, but not all. The large differences between why both countries departed the ERM produced significant differences in outcomes.

The major depreciation of the pound allowed the UK to return to growth. In Italy, most things got worse.

Soon after I joined Moody's in 1992, I became the lead analyst for a number of EU institutions, such as the European Union itself, the European Coal and Steel Community, the Council of Europe, the European Investment Bank, among others. Given this portfolio, I regularly traveled to Brussels and Luxembourg to meet with the staffs of these institutions.

With the ERM crisis recent in everyone's mind, there were many discussions during meals about the decision to forge ahead with a common currency, following a specific timeline.

These technocrats were quite frank about the reason for creating a common currency. They were the first people to tell me about the importance of the agreement between Kohl and Mitterrand. It was obvious to them that it was purely political, not economic. As time passed, EU bureaucrats felt less at liberty to criticize the almost religious devotion to creating the euro. They knew there would be serious problems that wouldn't or couldn't be easily fixed.

Their only hope was that Italy would not qualify for membership. If Italy could be kept out, they thought there was a chance that the differences between the French, German and Benelux economies would allow the new currency to function adequately.

Little did anyone predict that Italians were willing to make a gargantuan effort to qualify. Special taxes were enacted, expenses were curtailed, and pension reforms were passed. Then the disaster happened for the euro and Italy. In 1998, Italy met the so-called *convergence criteria* and joined on the first day electronic euro came into existence. There were eleven original members of this club. Greece hadn't even been thought to be in the running for Eurozone membership because the economic convergence criteria looked impossible for it to meet. As we would learn in subsequent years, Greek statistics proved quite easy to manipulate, eventually causing the Greek crisis of recent years.

Once the euro was created, and eventually eclipsed the former local currencies in 2002, it seemed it could easily work for a number of years. A crisis would have to wait.

Eurozone (EZ) central banks may provide liquidity to their own banks, with the only requirement being that they inform Frankfurt (where the ECB is headquartered) about the injection of liquidity so Frankfurt could undertake monetary operations to counter that liquidity creation if it wished. During normal times, such a system worked. However, the depth of the crisis ended business as usual.

The size of liquidity injections needed wasn't related to providing liquidity to just one or two banks, but to an entire banking system. Any such operation would pose significant risks to the ECB itself. In the end, the ECB handled the liquidity crisis by increasing the range of collateral it would accept, but it was clear that without further measures, the EZ might collapse.

We know the EZ didn't collapse, but the suffering brought about by the common currency reverberates to this day. In the real world, I now recognize that although the euro is terrible for countries such as Italy and Greece, the euro is too entrenched to be discarded, as I had hoped in its early years. The EU is tied to a totally inefficient mechanism to transfer gains from those countries advantaged by the euro, such as Germany, France and the Benelux to countries adversely affected countries such as Italy, Greece, Spain and Portugal.

A number of years ago, I did a study comparing how much money would need to be transferred to Italy every year from EZ countries, not as loans, but as grants in order to mimic Canada's interprovincial transfer mechanism. In Canada, wealthy provinces transfer money to poorer provinces. This helps keep the Canadian federation and monetary union intact. Australia and Germany have similar mechanisms in place. In Italy itself, for over a century, the North has been sending money to the South to keep Italy together.

I calculated that about €30 billion would need to be transferred to Italy by other EZ countries to match the transfer mechanism in place in Canada, using Quebec as a proxy for Italy. Similarities between comparing Quebec to the whole of Canada and Italy to the whole of the EZ included the fact that both are relatively large compared to the whole, and are wealthy, but not as wealthy as some other monetary union members. Such sizable transfers from the EZ to Italy will never materialize. Therefore, the

EZ, no matter what is done to forge a closer union, will never be able to adequately compensate those countries disadvantaged by the monetary union. The sad truth is that EZ flaws cannot be fixed, only papered over.

Life After Moody's

I was getting exhausted from three decades of constant international travel. It wasn't the travel per se, but the time zone changes that slowly take their toll. I was looking for life beyond Moody's. After leaving Moody's, I assumed I would quickly move into a full retirement mode. Soon, I became bored. I joined a small asset management company, NewOak, where I worked part-time as a Managing Director. Then I was approached by Granite Springs Asset Management. There, I was initially a Managing Director and eventually became a partner. When Granite Springs was sold, I thought full-time retirement was about to begin. Wrong again.

INCRA

I was approached by the Bertelsmann Foundation North America), a large German foundation dedicated to strengthening Trans-Atlantic relations, to help put together a proposal on how to create a not-for-profit Sovereign Rating Agency. It was never the intention for the Foundation to open such an agency, but rather to provide a blueprint for those who might wish to pursue such a venture.

I was hooked. I wound up working on the project for several years on a part-time basis. Annette Heuser, the head of the Washington office, was a delight to work with, as was true for everyone involved with the Bertelsmann Foundation.

In the end, we produced one of the first ever sovereign rating methodologies based on easy to understand and explain inputs, including the specific weights assigned to each category. To see if the methodology worked, we had *mock credit committees*, which included experts from around the world, dedicated to *rating* national governments around the world. We had committees rate such countries as the US, France, Germany, Brazil and Japan. The methodology produced sovereign ratings similar to other CRAs, but which were far more quantitative and therefore easier to justify to the public.

When working on this project, once again, EU bureaucrats outdid themselves. The INCRA project (International Nonprofit Credit Rating Agency) was an academic undertaking. It was never meant to become a rating agency unless someone wished to use the template we provided, including estimates regarding costs.

After completing several ratings, INCRA organized a news conference in Berlin presenting the plan, including what kind of ratings it was capable of producing. These were never intended to be *real* ratings, but that's not how the ESMA (the European Securities and Markets Authority) regulators saw it. What appears to have happened when Annette Heuser didn't answer phone calls from Brussels, ESMA assumed that INCRA was violating EU regulations regarding rating agencies. The reason Ms. Heuser hadn't returned the phone call was that it was made during the Thanksgiving holiday weekend. For those who are familiar with German custom, emails and even phone calls are not answered over weekends and holidays. Therefore, it went unanswered. The result was that INCRA and the Bertelsmann Foundation were accused of violating EU ratings regulations. It wound up costing the foundation a lot of money in legal fees. Instead of carrying important foundation work, money had to be wasted because of overanxious regulators exerting their authority.

ACRA

Having worked on the INCRA project, I was contacted by people from Gazprombank about the possibility of helping to form a new Russian credit rating agency. At first, I laughed to myself – "a Russian rating agency?" I immediately thought of all the corruption Russian companies had become known for. I thought, no way! Then Ekaterina Trofimova, from Gazprombank, explained the plan in detail.

She understood credit rating agencies well after her years of experience at S&P. The biggest problem for a CRA in Russia, and elsewhere, is there can be not even a suspicion of a conflict of interest between the rating agency and issuers. The plan in Russia was to contact the 27 largest companies in Russia, with each injecting 3.7 percent of the capital. That way, no investor would hold sway in any rating outcomes. The list of companies providing initial capital is a *Who's Who* of the Russian economy. The list includes the biggest government-owned companies, the biggest government-owned financial institutions, the biggest privately-owned companies, which I was surprised to hear referred to as *Oligarch*-owned companies. Oligarch may be a pejorative term in the West, but in Russia, it is widely used as a descriptive, with no animus attached to the term. Large private banks and several foreign bank subsidiaries rounded out the shareholder base. To avoid the appearance of a potential conflict of interest, shareholders were restricted in selling shares. I was increasingly intrigued. A new Russian rating agency was becoming more doable.

Ekaterina explained that there was an issue with putting together an independent Board of Directors. The problem was that there are so few people with rating agency or similar experience anywhere in the world. On top of that, the pool was even smaller within Russia. Anyone they thought might be qualified was already sitting on other corporate boards, therefore presenting the appearance of a potential conflict of interest. The solution was to create a board entirely made up of foreigners. Ekaterina said all board-related activity would be conducted in English.

After learning who other potential board members were, I quickly agreed to become a board member for this new Russian rating agency. ACRA (Analytical Credit Rating Agency) was established at the end of 2015. The acronym was perfect because it was the same in Russian and English. Also, the word acra in Greek means summit, something we would aim for.

Thus, I began taking regular trips to Moscow, albeit nowhere near the number of times that I had traveled while at Moody's.

The staff of ACRA is incredibly talented. Almost all speak fluent English, plus a number speak several other languages. Most have advanced degrees, with many having the equivalent of a Ph.D. It has proved to be one of the most interesting undertakings I've ever done. Who would have thought that in retirement, I would be doing things more interesting than what I had done during my long career?

What has been exciting is that together we have created a world-class rating agency, that I would argue is equal in quality to the head offices of the big three rating agencies, all of this in less than three years.

Earlier, I described how depressing Moscow was in the late 1980's. Today, it is a modern metropolis, with fine shops and restaurants. GUM is now a shopping mall filled with top designer boutiques catering to the wealthy. The people no longer look sullen as they did during the Gorbachev years. Instead, they look like other Europeans dressed in the latest fashions. They don't smile as much as Americans, but then again, no one smiles as much as we do. I learned that smiling used to be frowned upon – please forgive the pun. One explanation was that most people's teeth were in bad shape, so no one wanted to smile. One Russian told me that when she was a teenager, she had to practice smiling in front of a mirror, because it was so alien and unnatural to smile. She learned well.

Crime against foreigners is nearly non-existent, a total change from the 80s and early 90s. If you haven't been to Moscow, I would highly recommend a visit. Whenever I visit for board meetings, my stay is short and filled with business activities. On one such trip, I extended my stay, so my son could join me. We spent about an extra week touring Moscow.

When on business, I stay at a normal business hotel. For the vacation portion of that trip, my son and I stayed at the Kempinski, a hotel well known since Imperial times and more importantly, directly across from the Kremlin. The view from our windows was incredible. The Kremlin, St. Basil's Cathedral and the other churches on Red Square were just a short distance away on the other side of the Moscow River. Another WOW moment!

Since I had seen many Moscow landmarks on my first trip in the 1980s, and since at that time, walking was difficult for me, I arranged for my son to have a guided tour by a knowledgeable guide, similar to what I would do when visiting a city for the first time.

My son was, as usual, slightly late in meeting the guide. So, she and I sat in the hotel lobby and chatted a while about Russia. The Western European migrant crisis was in full swing. She then said that such a thing would never be allowed in Russia. She then went on to talk about Muslims living in Moscow, which makes up about 10 percent of population. She said we have no problems with our Muslim neighbors, but they must know that this is our country, not theirs. She went on that at New Year's, the Russian tradition is to toast the New Year with sparkling wine. She said that Muslims were expected to join in this tradition, even if it meant drinking alcohol. This was certainly a different attitude from the West, where we practically fawn over our minorities. This indicated that Orthodox culture will continue to thrive.

I have found Russia to be much more religious than I ever would have expected. New churches have appeared all over. The relationship between church and state is strong, like it used to be in the West. There are many Orthodox Christian shows on TV. On one trip, I was there for the Epiphany, which is different than the Western Epiphany. For us, the Epiphany is when the Three Wise Men visit the Baby Jesus. For Orthodox Christians, the Epiphany is the Feast of the Baptism of the Lord, about a week later than the Western holiday (or at least January 6 used to be a holiday).

The tradition is for devout Christians, who are able to, are to dip themselves three times in water, in a river, lake or ocean. Since the Feast occurs in the dead of winter, a bit of training is needed by those intending to participate. In ACRA, in that year, there were several young men who took part in that ceremony. You could also watch Putin do the same thing on TV.

Further evidence of religiosity was when I was there during Lent. We had a dinner party for shareholders. Many menu items had small crosses next to them. I was told that these items were *Lent-compliant*. It seemed everyone only ate Lent-compliant food. It wasn't just at that dinner party where I saw such a menu. The same crosses were on every restaurant menu, including the hotel where I was staying, which is owned by a Muslim.

All this reminded me of pre-Vatican II Christianity. I doubt the West was improved by that Church Council. For me, Vatican II represents one of the greatest blunders in Western history.

On that trip with my son, we only took the metro once, heading towards Gorky Park. I told him he had to see the Moscow metro, with its ornate stations built well-below the ground, which served as important bomb shelters during WW II.

It was a little difficult navigating the metro because almost all signs were in Cyrillic, sometimes making it difficult for me to quickly read cognates, which is always useful whenever dealing with a Latin script language.

We looked a bit lost. Then a young man walked over to us and asked where we wanted to go. He told us he was an American teaching at a university in Moscow. He kindly got us on the right train. He accompanied us for a few subway stops. He said it should be easier in the future for foreigners to navigate the metro because English language signs were being installed slowly throughout the system. That would certainly be a boon to foreign tourism.

Moscow is very spread out city. However, no matter how many times, and going to many places by car, I never saw slums. Finally, I asked, why? I was told by several people that there were no slums in the Western sense. One vestige of the Soviet Union is that everyone has a human right to housing. The housing may not be great, but you won't be left on the street.

It was pointed out that there were many buildings where people might still share kitchens, soviet style. They might be right next door to luxury condominiums. I guess another important reason is that you are homeless in most of Russia during the winter, you'd be dead. It's too cold. There might be beggars, but I have never seen any. Unlike during the end of Communism and during the early days after the collapse, crime was endemic. It was a dangerous place. Today, crimes against foreigners in Moscow are almost non-existent.

I have found the reaction of my friends at home to be entertaining. I'm always told to be careful when going to Moscow. I just smile.

Anti-Russian sentiment in the US is over-the-top. Putin has been made out to be a *villain extraordinaire*. In Russia, although he has less support in major urban areas like Moscow and St. Petersburg, his support is strong across the country's heartland. Sound familiar?

Russians remember the chaos after the fall of Communism. Falling real wages, crime, shortages of everything, shocking changes to everyday life come one upon the other. We may debate why Yeltsin chose Putin to replace him, but the reality is that for Russians, most things got better quickly. Whether by design or by the good fortune of higher energy prices, life under Putin has been much better for most Russians. The same can't be said for Greeks, Italians or Brazilians, among others.

The Ukraine, Crimea and Syria

I believe Russia has been misunderstood. Well before joining ACRA, I wrote a number of blogs about the Ukraine, Crimea and Syria. I have had a contrarian views of all three for a number of years.

The Crimea is the most important. Before 1954, Crimea was never part of the Ukraine. It was *suddenly* given to the Ukraine by Khrushchev. The transfer was only announced once in Pravda, eight days after the fact. There were no follow up articles. The most likely explanation for the transfer involved infighting among Soviet leaders. Stalin had died one year earlier. Three men were vying for that role: Malenkov, Beria and Khrushchev.

The problem Khrushchev faced was his role in the Ukrainian civil war following the expulsion of the Nazis.

Many Ukrainians resisted returning to the Soviet Union and demanded independence. Khrushchev crushed that rebellion but at great cost in Ukrainian lives. To get support from senior Ukrainian Communists in the post-Stalinist USSR, the transfer of Crimea to the Ukraine is seen by some as a kind of *goodwill* gesture. Others say it was because of his *fondness* for the Ukraine. A plethora of other reasons are hypothesized. In the end, no one knows for sure, but it definitely came out of the blue, and ran contrary to 171 years of Russian history.

Crimea has been Russia's traditional naval base in the Black Sea. The idea that Russia would give that up to the Ukraine is absurd, especially since some Ukrainians are demanding membership in NATO.

The establishment of the Soviet Union in 1917 caused major strife throughout the Ukraine, so much so that the capital of the Ukraine couldn't be moved back to Kiev until 1934. Western Ukrainians, predominantly Roman Catholic and Eastern Ukrainians, more often Russian Orthodox, have been at loggerheads for centuries. When examining historical voting patterns, the country is neatly divided between Western and Eastern Ukraine.

The treatment of Russian speakers in the Eastern Donbass region remains a serious problem, not likely to go away anytime soon.

Syria is a complicated problem, most of which is based on demographics. The Syrian population is quite diverse.

Although overwhelmingly Arab, there are small but important Armenian, Kurdish and Turkmen communities.

Religiously, the country is even more diverse. Prior to the civil war, Sunni Arabs made up an estimated 43-44% of the population, Sunni Kurds accounted for about 10%, Sunni Turkmen for about 3-5%, Alawites accounted for about 12%, about 10%-13% Christian, non-Alawite Shiites about 4% and Druze 3%.

I don't want to get into the theological debate surrounding where the Alawites stand within the Muslim community, except to say, they were traditionally viewed as *heretics* by most Muslims. More recently, Alawites were given recognition as Shiites by leading Iranian clerics.

Recognition of Alawites as Shiite is seen as a gift from the late Ayatollah Khomeini, who had been given refuge by Assad's father prior to the Iranian Revolution of 1979.

The irony is that before the so-called Arab Spring, Assad was reforming the country, both economically and politically. In the end, the Arab Spring caused the Syrian Civil War. There hasn't been a single country that benefitted from the Arab Spring. It has proved a disaster for the Arab world.

Assad was able to keep the communities peaceful. He was viewed as the protector of the Alawites, Christians and the small Jewish community. He was, and is, far from perfect, but the result of the civil war is worse than anyone could have imagined.

For decades Syria provided the Soviet Union, and now Russia, with a large Mediterranean naval base in Latakia. As with Crimea, Russia is not going to give up such an important military installation. In addition, with Russia's Orthodox resurrection, Russia had resumed its historical role as the protector of Christians in the Middle East. Beside maintaining a military presence in Latakia, protecting Christians represent another reason Russia has helped Assad.

Paul Kazarian

About five years ago, I got a call from Paul Kazarian. He asked me to meet with him and Ian Ball to talk about government accounting. That meeting changed my view of how to look at government financial statistics.

I had always looked at government finance through an economist's eyes. They pointed out how much proper accounting could help improve government transparency and efficiency through FRSB and IPSAS-based accounting. I had been presented with some of these ideas when I was the lead analyst for New Zealand. Ian had become well-known for his role in the implementation New Zealand's reforms. I have to be frank, at the time, the ideas sounded interesting, but as soon as we got to traditional accounting, I guess I let those concepts go over my head, paying them little mind.

The reason for the meeting was related to accounting, but specifically to the EZ crisis, in particular, how it had affected Greece and the Greek people, and how the country's plight might be lifted.

Paul, who is a brilliant and successful businessman, was shocked that Greek government accounting was totally out of line with FRSB and IPSAS-based accounting. In our discussion, I had pointed out my criticism of Eurostat (the EU's statistical arm) handling of debt. It made no sense even in economic terms. The rules in place by Maastricht forced government to report debt, even when rescheduled, at the face amount of the debt, not the NPV, the net present value of the debt. I had written blogs about the problem with Greek debt reporting.

What Paul and Ian showed me was that even things like NPV are inadequate to measure debt. In addition, if governments adopt IPSAS-based accounting at the national level, the ability of governments to make sound judgements based on actual costs. Transparency about the effect of government fiscal policy is much enhanced. Transparency will move governments in the direction of improving efficiency. If not, then that government will likely be ousted in the next national election.

Paul undertook it upon himself, with the help of his staff, to approximate what the Greek debt actually looked like if normal accounting practices were used. The difference was huge. On top of estimating the debt, accounting always requires entities to calculate their assets. In other words, he produced an estimate of the Greek government's balance sheet.

The end result was not only did Greek government debt fall dramatically, but when financial assets were added to the mix, the net debt of the Greek government, relative to GDP was not a horrific 175 percent of GDP. Instead, the debt/GDP ratio fell to ???, with the net debt/GDP ratio being one of the lowest in the EU.

As we have learned in studying physics, how you look at something can have an effect on the outcome. Using FRSB and IPSAS accounting resulted in showing the Greek government wasn't in disastrous financial shape. Rather, it was in reasonably good shape.

I was hooked on the idea of spreading these concepts to fellow economists, especially those in rating agencies, governments and IFIs. Without using traditional accounting, the true financial picture of a government might easily be distorted.

Paul asked me to participate in a number of conferences. After several years, after he established the Kazarian Center for Public Financial Management (KCPFM), he asked me to be one of its Senior Advisors, something I continue to do.

Maxxsure

In addition, I am a Senior Advisor for Maxxsure, a cybersecurity firm headquartered in Texas. It's a great company which is expanding rapidly. Over the years, Shawn Wiora and Srik Soogoor co-CEOs of Maxxsure and I have become good friends. My role is to help provide input into layering on country risk on their already very sophisticated cybersecurity models. If you had told me years ago that I would be involved in cybersecurity, I would have laughed.

St. James' Church

I should add that besides working with ACRA and KCPFM, I am also active in my local church, where I serve as Treasurer. I am proud that St. James' Episcopal Church, in Long Branch, New Jersey, a small mission church, is able to feed between 1200-1500 people a month, providing hot meals and groceries three times a week, almost entirely staffed by volunteers.

There is always still more to do. I intend to keep trying as long as God allows. My advice to everyone is: **Don't just sit there! Do something!** It will make life far more fulfilling.

www.ingramcontent.com/pod-product-compliance
Lightning Source LLC
Chambersburg PA
CBHW020628220526
45464CB00001B/68